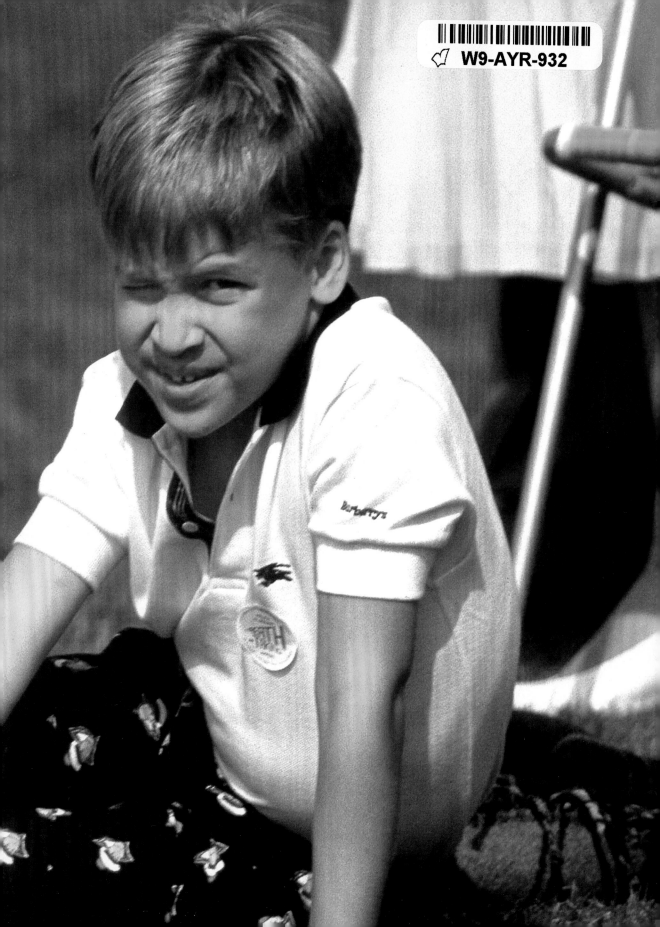

Prince

William

Other books by the author:

Princess Anne
Monarchy
Invitation to the Palace
Anne: The Princess Royal
The New Royal Court
All the Queen's Men
The Queen and Her Family
Maclean of Duart
Mountbatten: The Private Story
Anne: The Private Princess Revealed
Buckingham Palace: A Guide
Diana: Princess of Wales
Charles & Diana – Portrait of a Marriage
The Royal Yacht Britannia
Her Majesty – Fifty Regal Years
Queen Elizabeth II – 50 Years Jubilee Edition
At Home With The Queen

Prince William

Brian Hoey

SUTTON PUBLISHING

First published in 2003 by
Sutton Publishing Limited · Phoenix Mill
Thrupp · Stroud · Gloucestershire · GL5 2BU

British Library Cataloguing in Publication Data
A catalogue record of this book is available from the British Library.

ISBN 0 7509 3265 1

Endpapers, *front:* Seven-year-old William, unconsciously advertising his fashionable Burberry polo shirt, at Smith's Lawn, Guards Polo Club, Windsor, July 1989; *rear:* During his gap year William joined the Raleigh International expedition to Chile, where he enjoyed working with local communities – and where moments of relaxation were rare and precious.

Typeset in 10/16½ pt Eurostile.
Typesetting and origination by
Sutton Publishing Limited.
Printed and bound in England by
J.H. Haynes & Co. Ltd, Sparkford.

For

Laurence, Rebecca and Jessica

As a member of Eton's elite Pop Society William was allowed to wear waistcoats of his own choice. This one made in the design of the Union Jack shows his patriotic leanings – and was popular with his fellow prefects.

Contents

William has often said that when he is in Scotland he is quite happy to spend a few hours alone except for the company of a dog. He is seen here on the banks of the River Dee at Balmoral.

Acknowledgements

The main difficulty in writing about any living member of the Royal Family is that the subject rarely gives interviews to authors. There have been exceptions, of course. I myself received a great deal of cooperation from the Princess Royal when I was compiling her biography, and Prince Charles allowed an authorized biography to be written that included personal comments and quotations. But these are the exception rather than the rule. So when I began preparing this book about Prince William, I knew from the outset that I would not be able to rely on family members for information about him.

Instead I spoke to a number of people who have known the Prince throughout his life, some of whom are present and former members of the Royal Household and the Royalty Protection Department who, for obvious reasons, allowed me to do so on condition that I respected their anonymity. I am glad to express my appreciation of their help. I would also like to thank the Duchess of Westminster, one of William's godparents, the Rt Hon. Chris Patten PC, Lord Blake, arguably Britain's foremost expert on constitutional monarchy, Mr Mohamed Al Fayed, who played host to William and Harry and their late mother, Princess Diana, on their last holiday together, Chester Stern, Philip Gosling and Captain Norman Lloyd-Edwards, Lord Lieutenant of South Glamorgan, who kindly gave me so much time and provided me with a couple of personal pictures. Jayne Fincher was the first photographer to be invited to take official pictures of William and I am grateful to her for the anecdotes of the many occasions they were together. I was fortunate to be able to speak to a former fellow student of William's at St Andrews, Lizzie Hadley, while the editor of New Zealand *Womens' Weekly* gave me permission to quote from an extensive interview she had obtained with Lizzie. The Prince of Wales's office supplied me with certain factual information regarding Prince William.

The majority of photographs in the book have been provided by Anwar Hussein and Jayne Fincher, both of whom have distinguished reputations as Royal photographers. Mr Hussein's photographs are on pp. i, vi, xi, xii, xiii, xix, xx, 1, 2, 6, 8, 9, 12, 17, 19, 22–3, 25, 26, 27, 28, 31, 33, 34, 36, 37, 40, 43, 44, 45, 47, 48, 49, 51, 53, 55, 56, 58, 60, 62, 63, 64, 68 (top), 71, 73, 74, 82, 84 (top), 87, 88, 90, 91, 92, 93, 94, 95, 96, 97, 99, 100, 102, 103, 104, 106, 107, 108, 109, 114, 117, 119, 121, 122–3, 125, 126, 128, 129, 130–1, 132, 133, 134, 135, 136, 137, 139, 140, 141, 142, 143, 145, 146, 147, 148, 150, 152, 156, 158, 159, 168, 169, 176, 177, 178, 180, 182, 183, 184, 186–7, 190, 192, rear endpaper. Ms Fincher's photographs are on the front endpaper, pp. viii, xv, xvi, xvii, xviii, 4–5, 20, 38, 39, 42, 50, 57, 68 (bottom), 70, 75, 76, 78, 79, 84 (bottom), 120, 127, 160, 161, 163, 164, 166, 172–3, 181. I am also grateful to the following sources of illustrations: Rex Features (pp. 14, 18, 154); *Western Mail* (pp. 61, 65, 67); BCA Film Ltd (p. 188); European Commission Audiovisual Library (p. 111); Russell West (p. 77).

At Sutton Publishing I have been greatly encouraged by Darryl Reach, while the expertise of Jeremy Yates-Round and Peter Clifford really got the project off the ground. Jaqueline Mitchell has been a constant source of energy with her inventive suggestions, while Alison Miles has edited the book with perceptive skill and deceptive speed, managing both to improve my original text and keep my nose to the grindstone. Helen Holness has had the responsibility for marketing the book. My wife Diana gave me much help in checking the text, while Mike Shaw and Jonathan Pegg at Curtis Brown are all too aware of how much I owe them. I am glad to have this opportunity of acknowledging my debt publicly and to all of them I offer my gratitude with the usual qualification that, except where attributed, all opinions – and any errors – are mine and mine alone.

Brian Hoey
February 2003

Acknowledgements

Introduction

Sometime this century, Prince William of Wales will be crowned King William V. Nothing is more certain. It is as inevitable as night follows day and a situation William could not change, even if he wanted to. Reports that Prince Charles might step aside in favour of his elder son are based on nothing more than ill-informed speculation without a glimmer of truth. It is never going to happen. The idea that Prince Charles might give up his place in the line of succession in order to marry Camilla Parker Bowles is a complete non-starter. Once we follow that route, the whole principle of an hereditary monarchy is finished. Charles, if he survives The Queen, will be our next King and his elder son will follow him. In any event, it would not be up to him to offer the throne to William even if he wanted to relinquish his own position.

Lord Blake, Britain's foremost authority on the monarchy and the constitution, says 'Charles's whole life has been geared to the assumption that he will be King. There is not the slightest evidence from anyone that he has any intention of giving it up. And even if he wanted to turn the throne over to William, the choice of succession is not his to make. Parliament would have to agree to allow Charles to leave, then select a new King, and that could throw the entire idea of monarchy open to official and possibly acrimonious debate.'

Prince Charles has said that he hated not being allowed to have even the smallest say in the direction his life was to follow: 'You can't understand what it is like to have your whole life mapped out for you. It's so awful to be programmed.'

Opposite: *William was persuaded to join his father and brother for this family photograph outside the main entrance of Highgrove in July 1999.*

Right: *William says his favourite holidays are at Balmoral. Here he is on the banks of the River Dee in the summer of 1997 getting ready to fish.*

And William, above all others of his contemporaries, knows exactly what his destiny is: he is going to be King. There is no other role for him. He may be allowed to spend periods in the armed forces, or undertake socially acceptable tasks in the Third World, but all will be strictly supervised, the people with whom he will work specially chosen and every aspect of his career will have but one solitary aim: to make him suitable as a future sovereign. William's father has had the same on-going training as a 'King-in-Waiting' for over fifty years, and his grand-mother, Queen Elizabeth II, knew from the age of ten, when her uncle abdicated as King Edward VIII and her father was suddenly propelled from being a comparatively obscure Duke of York into the limelight of ascending the throne as King George VI, that she too had no control over her future. She was heir presumptive and accepted without question that she would one day become Queen. There was no alternative, and where Royalty is concerned things have not changed all that much in the last 200 years. The hereditary principle being what it is, William knows that, barring accidents, he will become His Majesty King William V.

Prince William of Wales – he will be recognized as His Royal Highness only on his twenty-first birthday, when it is also possible he will be made a Knight of the Thistle – could have become HRH when he was eighteen, but he did not want this and his father persuaded The Queen to delay the honorific title. He is also the only student at his, or any other, university (with the possible exception of President Clinton's daughter Chelsea) who is required to wear an electronic 'panic button' at all times. When he was leaving Eton, a group of his fellow sixth formers grabbed the security device and threw it in the Thames. William saw the joke even if his royal bodyguards didn't.

Introduction

In many ways he is a very ordinary young man who has found himself in an extraordinary situation, unique even. No other person of his generation has had to make the transition from Royal splendour, living in palaces and castles one minute, to being just one of 6,000 students at a provincial university the next. It has not come easily and he still faces problems in coming to terms with being a member of a family whose every peccadillo is chronicled in minute detail. The last year has been particularly difficult with Royal scandal following Royal scandal, highly publicized court cases collapsing through The Queen's personal intervention and members of Prince Charles's household being involved in unconventional activities. If William has managed to maintain a sense of *savoir-faire* through all these tribulations somebody must have done something right in his early days.

'The one thing his father and I were absolutely agreed on was that William would have as normal an upbringing as possible', the words of the late Diana, Princess of Wales, speaking about her first child. It was an understandable and commendable wish but normal is a description that is difficult to understand when applied to almost any member of the Royal Family, particularly when it concerns someone on whom so many hopes are pinned. William is the star of the future, the one whom The Queen and the Duke of Edinburgh believe will take the monarchy safely into the years ahead. And what can be normal when you realize that this particular son cannot fly in the same aircraft with his father in case an accident should deprive the nation of two future sovereigns. Or that when he first started at nursery school William was not allowed to know its name 'for security reasons', which must have seemed a mystery to this little three-year-old pupil. Even today, and for the foreseeable future, his every movement is controlled by Royal protocol.

No other young man in the world bears the burden of having his mother, the most famous woman in the world, killed in a horrific car crash with her lover, his father involved in what was arguably the most publicized love affair of the century, a grandmother who is also his Queen and a great-grandfather who was the last Emperor of India. So normal is hardly the word that immediately springs to mind when describing William's background and life so far.

William has never been able to lose himself or suddenly take off and spend a couple of days – or even hours – alone, without informing his police 'minders' where he is going – and he will not be able to for the rest of his life. Prince Charles has insisted that neither of his sons take part in Royal duties until they

This picture of the Princess of Wales and her two sons was taken in the garden of Highgrove in August 1988.

have completed their education. In an interview William gave at Highgrove he said, 'My father wants me to finish full-time education before doing Royal duties and so do I. It will be a few years before I do royal engagements although I expect, as in the past, I will sometimes accompany my father.'

The Prince has the Royals' natural suspicion of being taken advantage of and goes out of his way to avoid the possibility. He claims his mother was exploited by many men and women (and some might say that she also did a fair amount of manipulating herself) and believes her image still is.

Keenly aware of his position in the Royal line-up, the apparently shy and sometimes introspective William remains what most people regard as the classic first child and older brother. He likes being the one to look out for Harry and, since the death of their mother, regards himself as the one to whom Harry can look for unqualified support. There is a common bond between the two boys, particularly as each knows better than anyone else the problems the other faces in growing up as part of the most famous family in the world. But whereas Harry is the more easy-going of the two, even at his age realizing that he is unlikely ever to have to face the responsibilities of William, he does occasionally show his frustration at being 'tail-end Charlie' all the time. He is never going to attract the same amount of attention William gets now and will

Right: *Prince William, holding his father's hand, arrives at the Lindo Wing of St Mary's Hospital in Paddington, London, to see his new baby brother, Harry, for the first time, June 1984.*

Opposite: *The nine-month-old Prince William is carried by his nanny, Barbara Barnes, as they arrive at Heathrow Airport prior to boarding a flight to Australia in March 1983. They are watched by one of the armed Royalty Protection officers whose gun is clearly visible as his jacket swings open.*

continue to receive throughout his life, and Harry does not always relish the thought of being overshadowed. He is at an age where he feels the need to prove himself and there is a healthy sibling rivalry. But William enjoys his position and leaves his brother in no doubt about who is number one.

William has a self-deprecating sense of fun among his friends and family – even sharing his mother's love of risqué jokes – but can be caustic towards the press, which he hates. He has inherited many of the characteristics of his grandfather Prince Philip: a love of sport, particularly shooting – though he obeyed his mother when she advised him, with an eye on political correctness, not to be photographed holding a shotgun in his hands – and riding. Like Prince Philip (and the Princess Royal), William has a quick temper and short fuse and does not suffer fools gladly. His aggressive attitude towards photographers has been demonstrated several times when he has apparently ridden straight at them if he feels they are being too intrusive when he is out hunting. But he also follows Prince Charles in the manner in which he likes his life to be ordered and planned, accepting without question the deference of Royal servants and demanding total and instant obedience. The staff at all Royal residences know that when William 'requests' something, he wants it immediately – excuses are not tolerated. So while physically the resemblance with his late mother is uncanny, with his height, fair hair and blue eyes all coming from the Spencer family, his character is very much a product of the House of Windsor. He is Royal through and through.

The Prince's pastimes are predominately upper class. Hunting with the fashionable meets near his father's Gloucestershire home, joining shooting weekend parties at Sandringham and at other country houses in the shires and exclusive dinner parties where an unwritten code of '*omertà*' exists to protect Royal guests from appearing in tabloid gossip columns. Nobody breaks the code twice. They know that when the Royal curtain descends, it is with chilling finality.

Prince Charles has emerged as a successful single parent in the years since Diana's death and the family circle now includes Camilla Parker Bowles, Charles's long-time companion. William and Harry have accepted her, not as a surrogate mother, but as a 'non-negotiable' part of Charles's life (his words), and if her presence pleases him they are content for her to be around. They want him to be happy; it makes their lives easier, and if Camilla is what it takes, they are prepared to maintain the appearance of being a united family unit. Any disagreements over her position have been resolved and a compromise reached.

Perhaps the most poignant view anyone has had of William was at the funeral of his mother, the late Diana, Princess of Wales. Walking with his brother Harry

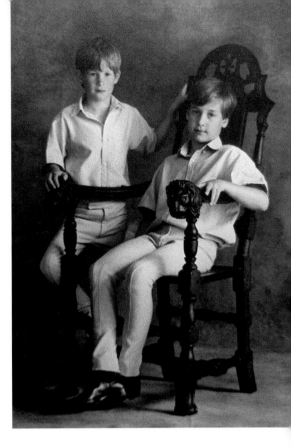

Right: *An early Christmas card showing Prince Harry standing alongside his older brother William. It is said to have been one of their parents' favourite pictures.*

Opposite: *Surely the happiest photograph ever taken on board the Royal Yacht* Britannia. *The Princess of Wales greets her sons after their flight from England to join her in Toronto, Canada, in October 1991, and the joy is plain to see.*

and Diana's brother, Earl Spencer, their eyes cast down, while Prince Charles and the Duke of Edinburgh held their heads high, few could fail to have been moved as the youngest princes in the Royal Family kept their emotions firmly under control. Their bearing was impeccable and showed a maturity way beyond their years. It was an exercise in Royal discipline that William had learned from an early age and one that he will remember all his life.

The boys repeated the exercise five years later for the funeral of their great-grandmother, Queen Elizabeth, the Queen Mother. This was a full Royal ceremonial occasion with nearly 2,000 troops on parade, military bands playing and Her Majesty's coffin borne on a gun-carriage pulled by six horses of the King's Troop, Royal Horse Artillery in a perfect blend of poignancy and pomp. The Royal party walked in the procession from St James's Palace to the Palace of Westminster where the Queen Mother lay in state for three-and-a-half days, and when the formal proceedings were over, William and Harry remained for a few moments to pay their own private respects. It was yet another part of their Royal training and this time it was they who were supporting their father who had been particularly close to his grandmother. As she was 101 years old when she died there obviously was not the sense of loss that accompanied the

Prince William was confirmed on 9 March 1997. This official portrait, taken in the White Drawing Room at Windsor Castle, includes in the front row, alongside William, Prince Harry, the Prince and Princess of Wales and The Queen. Standing are his surviving godparents, from left to right: King Constantine, Lady Susan Hussey, Princess Alexandra, the Duchess of Westminster and Lord Romsey.

sudden death of Princess Diana in 1997. Sadness yes, but no great wave of national emotion as the Royal Family and the nation bade farewell. For William it was an occasion to appear as a controlled adult, which he did with perfect solemnity. His great-grandmother would have been proud of his natural Royal bearing. She would also have understood when he decided not to attend the memorial service for Princess Margaret because his term at university had just started and he did not want to interrupt his studies. There was no snub intended. He behaved as he felt he should and in doing so he had the full approval of The Queen and Prince Charles.

William is already fully aware that, as eventual heir to the throne, his future life will be dictated by public duty and the expectations of an affectionate but demanding people. He can have few illusions about what that means and the course of his life for the foreseeable future.

one
A Day in the
Life of . . .

Whether it is in term time at university, at weekends or at home on holiday, William is an early riser. He is woken every morning at 7.30. At Highgrove, Balmoral, Sandringham and St James's Palace, a footman brings him a 'calling tray' on which is placed a pot of coffee and a few biscuits. The coffee is served in a bone-china cup and saucer and he drinks it black with no sugar. The footman enters his bedroom quietly, though William is often already awake. He places the tray on a table beside the bed, turns on the radio, which is tuned to BBC Radio Four as William likes to hear the news, and then draws back the heavy curtains.

William does not like to lie around in bed, and within minutes he rises to shave and shower – and to complete his Canadian Air Force exercises, which he religiously does every morning before breakfast. While he is drinking his coffee, one of his father's three valets lays out the clothes that William will be wearing, having brought them from the large wardrobe where his outfits are kept. The valet will have been given a copy of the day's programme the evening before, so he knows which outfits to prepare. He doesn't ask which shirt and tie he wants to wear, saying that is what he is paid to decide. If William intends riding that morning, his kit – jodhpurs, check shirt, hacking jacket and highly polished boots – is laid out ready to be donned after breakfast; he goes down to the dining room – breakfast is never served in bed – wearing jeans and a sweater. At home in Highgrove, breakfast is served in the dining room, and

while there is always a 'full English' on offer, William rarely eats anything more than a bowl of cereal with cold milk and some fresh fruit.

In the Prince's flat at St Andrews, there is no footman or housemaid, and the three young men and one young woman who share the apartment take it in turns to make the coffee. If they are lucky, William's police bodyguard might already have made it. When he lived in hall at St Andrews, he could virtually fall out of bed and into the dining hall downstairs, where he sat with whoever happened to be up and about. William is not a great conversationalist first thing in the morning. And although he usually stuck to his healthy diet, one of his fellow students said he did occasionally enjoy 'two bacon butties and a mug of tea'.

After returning to his room to brush his teeth, William joins his fellow students who are taking History of Art in the first of the day's lectures. At weekends, if he is remaining in St Andrews and not dashing off to Balmoral, he and a couple of his closest friends will stroll into town to buy newspapers and have a coffee. At Highgrove, Prince Charles usually has the day planned. He does not like the idea of anyone lying around and doing nothing and he expects his sons to comply with his suggestions. As these often include riding, William and Harry are all too willing to fall in with their father's plans. They enjoy anything to do with horses and the stables at Highgrove are well equipped both for them and for any of their friends who may have been invited for the weekend. Those who are asked to stay overnight find a curious mixture of delightful informality and Royal correctness. One young friend who was invited to Highgrove for the first time, asked William what he should bring in the way of clothes. 'Oh nothing too grand,' he was told, 'just throw in a pair of jeans and a dinner jacket.'

Opposite: *William at St Andrews University in Scotland in September 2001, having enrolled for a four-year degree course in the History of Art.*

Overleaf: *Highgrove, the Prince of Wales's country home in Gloucestershire, is where William likes to relax and where he can enjoy total privacy and security. His rooms are said to be sacrosanct, furnished in his own style and to his own tastes.*

William loves driving and particularly enjoys taking his off-road motor bike over the fields and through the woods at Highgrove. Having passed his stage two motor-cycle test on 2 January 2002, he now also likes riding around the country lanes near his father's house without L plates. The Prince was taught to drive a car by Sergeant Chris Gilbert, one of the Metropolitan Police Force's most experienced instructors, at the Police Driving School at Hendon. There William learned to handle a vehicle on the skid-pan, which he said was 'great fun' and also, something most drivers do not have included in their lessons, how to take evasive action if in danger of attack. Sergeant Gilbert said William was an enthusiastic pupil and he passed his driving test on 27 July 1999, just five weeks after his seventeenth birthday.

During the week, lunch at the university is taken in one of the dining rooms and is usually fairly plain. University food is like most institutional fare, heavy on starches, healthy but bland, with the occasional salad thrown in for good measure. William eats sparsely and potatoes and sticky puddings are kept to a minimum, though he has no need to diet. At 6 ft 2 in, he has plenty of room to put on a little weight if he wants to, but his natural metabolism ensures that he retains a trim figure. He also rarely drinks anything but spring water during the day. By the time he was fourteen, he had given up Coke for still water.

Afternoons at university are devoted to sport. William enjoys practically every kind of games activity, with soccer, rugby and swimming high on the list. St Andrews does not boast a polo team, so this great favourite has to wait until weekends and holidays.

Like most students, William does not care to wash his clothes himself. His wardrobe is large enough that he doesn't have to bother too much about wearing the same clothes every day. He normally throws all his dirty washing in a bag and takes it home at weekends for the staff to launder, and brings it back on Sunday evenings. There's not all that much difference between what the Prince does and all the others, except that with them it is usually their mother who does the chores. At Highgrove and St James's Palace, he doesn't have to lift a finger for himself. There are servants to attend to his every need.

Opposite: *One of William's great passions is polo, which he plays with courage and determination. He is seen here during the Porcelanosa Cup match at Ashe Park, Hampshire, in June 2002.*

At some time during the day, William attends to his correspondence. He is an assiduous letter writer and responds promptly to personal letters from friends and family. If he has spent the weekend as a guest at someone's house, he always writes a thank you note in his own hand, using a fountain pen, not the ballpoint he uses for lecture notes. He and Harry share a personal secretary, Helen Asprey (a member of the famous family of Crown Jewellers). She is based at St James's Palace as part of the Prince of Wales's office staff and handles all correspondence for the young princes. If she receives a letter with a coded initial in the lower left-hand corner she knows this is personal and from someone he knows, so sends it on to St Andrews, or wherever he happens to be, unopened. All official correspondence such as invitations to functions and requests for interviews are answered either by her or passed to the press office.

Among the skills Prince William acquired at Eton was how to make an omelette. But some of his classmates were not so sure of his culinary talents.

The two young princes, William and Harry, wearing the Golden Jubilee medals awarded to them by The Queen, leave St Paul's Cathedral after attending a service of thanksgiving to celebrate their grandmother's fifty years on the throne, June 2002.

Some of the letters border on the ridiculous, with dozens coming from love-sick teenagers who want a lock of William's hair, and even the occasional mother offering her daughter's hand in marriage. The letters are all kept safely just in case one might be from someone deranged and who could be a future threat. This is something all members of the Royal Family have had to live with. At Christmas and birthdays there's an avalanche of presents from women – not always young either – from all over the world. Each one receives an acknowledgement, but none is retained. Flowers are sent to local hospitals, toys are delivered to children's homes, but every box of chocolates, and there can be hundreds, is destroyed because of the possibility that the contents have been laced with poison. The same thing happens with the scores of Christmas and birthday cakes that well-meaning fans send in.

Now that William and his three flat mates are living independently of the campus, they tend to have their evening meal at one of the town's restaurants.

St Andrews likes to think of itself as something of a gourmet's paradise, so there's no shortage of places to choose from, with an abundance of Italian, French, Japanese, Chinese, Indian and Lebanese food on offer. William and his pals enjoy trying them out in turn, but they do not eat sophisticated meals every evening. Most nights a pizza or take-away is all they want. When they do go out, they share the cost of the meal with William paying his share. But he never uses his Coutts credit card in case someone sees the number and uses it without his knowledge, and also because he does not want to leave his signature where it might be sold as a souvenir. His police officer accompanies the party anyway, eating at a separate but nearby table, and on occasion he will pay the bill, claiming it back through his normal duty expenses later.

When he invites friends back to Highgrove or St James's Palace, William's hospitality approaches his father's legendary heights. Nothing is spared to make sure they have everything they want. He is a perfectionist, just like his father. Everything has to be just so and he personally inspects the rooms his guests are going to occupy, even making sure there is a supply of books by their favourite authors alongside their beds. He also checks the dinner table, even though he knows it will be perfect, making sure the seating plan is exactly the way he has arranged it. He prefers his dinner parties to be fairly small so that he can talk to everyone around the table and he likes to sit somewhere near the centre. When Prince Charles gives a dinner party, or attends one given by someone else, he always expects, and is accorded, a place at the head of the table. William goes to endless lengths to make sure his guests are comfortable and all the menus are chosen by him with the particular likes and dislikes of the party catered for.

William likes his fish poached not fried and his vegetables have to be crisp and not soggy, as is the usual British way. They also come from Prince Charles's home farm at Highgrove where they are organically grown. William prefers his meat to be cooked medium/rare and he particularly enjoys game, so venison is often on the menu. Pheasant under glass is another delicacy and, unlike Prince Charles, who drinks only white German burgundy, William enjoys a glass of claret as well as white wine. At dinner parties each place setting has five crystal glasses at its side: one each for white wine, with the first course, another for either red or white with the main course, a third for the sweet wine to accompany dessert, the fourth is for port or liqueurs, with the fifth reserved for water. He goes to enormous trouble to make sure his friends have a good time, and those who have never experienced Royal hospitality before leave feeling that they have had a wonderful evening and a unique experience. As one guest put it after dining with William, 'He turns an otherwise ordinary dinner party into a splendid occasion. He's a brilliant host.'

Weekdays at St Andrews tend not to go on too late. William is often in bed by 11 p.m., reading or watching a late film on television. The same routine is generally followed at Balmoral, when The Queen is in residence and William knows he has to be up early the next morning in readiness for the day's sport. But at home in Highgrove, things are much more relaxed and if he has been out to a local restaurant or pub, there's no set time for bed. Unless it is in the hunting season and he is going to be out very early, he often stays up well after midnight, playing records or talking to friends on his mobile. William is said to like the 'wee small hours' when the rest of the house is asleep and he can be alone with himself. It's not all that often that it happens. When it does he takes full advantage of the privacy and cherishes the time he is able to spend on his own.

But there is one major difference in William's day to that of his contemporaries. At some time he will spend an hour or two studying the papers The Queen and Prince Charles have sent him. These are not State papers, but documents and articles carefully selected that they believe will help him in his preparation for his eventual role as King. It's not a chore William enjoys, but one he knows his father undertook before him, and one he cannot ignore. His attitude to his future responsibilities already means that in spite of the comparative freedom he enjoys today, his monarchical homework must be done. And to his credit, the Prince has never complained about this encroachment on his personal life.

two
The Al Fayed
Connection

Mohamed Al Fayed describes the final weeks of Diana's life and how she, William and Harry came to be with his family just weeks before the fatal crash in a Paris underpass that killed her and his son Dodi:

It was very touching to see how close Diana was to her two sons. They were each given separate suites of course but when the maid took the early morning tea in she often found all three – Diana, William and Harry – tucked up in bed together, fast asleep. They were so vulnerable after the divorce that they needed the security of each other and loved nothing more than to cuddle up close. William was sixteen at the time, but there was nothing strange, sexual or unhealthy about it, it was just their way of showing their love for each other. They also used to have every meal sitting together and they swam, drove the jet-skis, in fact did everything together. I've never seen a mother and two teenage sons so close. They were inseparable.

Mr Al Fayed continues:

One day in July 1997, Diana rang me to say she and the boys needed a holiday and a little privacy. I have a house in the South of France and my yacht was there also so I told her it was hers for as long as she wanted it. 'I had known Diana and Charles for years. In fact all the Royal Family, ever since Prince Philip came to me to ask if I would sponsor the Royal Windsor Horse Show, which I did for over fifteen years. I have always respected The Queen. I used to talk with her and walk with her and she was always pleasant to me. I liked her very much and I still do – which is more than I can say for the rest of her family. The trouble with them is that they are still living in the past. They believe they are different from the rest of us and that they are still head of a great imperialist and colonial power.

Mohamed Al Fayed is the controversial figure who owns the most famous store in the world, Harrods, and who is equally well known for fighting the Establishment on every front. Never one to shrink from confrontation, he is afraid of nothing and no one, as he proved when he unveiled the shady deals and behind-the-scenes compromises that seem an inseparable part of British political life, revealing how MPs and other senior officials accepted – and expected – money and other expensive gifts for services rendered. He also controls Fulham Football Club and travels to his London headquarters every day by private helicopter from his country estate in Surrey, though he has several times been refused permission to land on the roof of Harrods. Without doubt the most high-profile businessman in Britain, he is a man of extraordinary energy and extreme generosity with a fair sprinkling of both friends and enemies in the highest places. He is on first-name terms with world leaders and Hollywood movie stars and counts sports celebrities such as David Beckham, and his wife Victoria, among his friends and acquaintances.

When Diana and Charles were divorced, it was the Princess who retained her close relationship with Mohamed and his family, while Prince Charles, the Duke of Edinburgh and the late Queen Mother all severed their connections with him. Where Royalty is concerned you are either for or against, and when Al Fayed refused to give up his friendship with Diana, they placed him firmly in the enemy camp. He claims it was not his decision to antagonize the Royal Family, he was simply not prepared to abandon Diana. She had already told him of her many battles with the Queen Mother describing her as '. . . an evil, evil woman, who went out of her way to make life difficult for me after the divorce'. Mohamed supported Diana as a lone parent and if this meant alienating the rest of the Royal Family, it was not something that bothered him, particularly as he was much more involved with the Spencers anyway: 'I had known Diana's father,

Dodi and Mohamed Al Fayed were friends with Diana and her children for years before the fatal accident in 1997. Here they are seen at a polo match at Smith's Lawn, Windsor, in July 1988.

Johnnie, for many years. He was one of my best friends, a very loving man, and Raine, his second wife, who nursed him back to health after his stroke, is still on the board of Harrods. That's how much I think of her.'

After Diana's telephone call in July 1997, Mohamed Al Fayed placed his house on the French Riviera at her disposal and offered it to her exclusively if she did not want any of his family there at the same time. 'I thought she might prefer to have the place to herself, but she wouldn't hear of it. She said she loved my wife and kids and she wanted us all to be there – one big happy family.' During the two weeks that Diana and her sons stayed with Mohamed, William spoke quite regularly to his host about his maternal grandfather, Earl Spencer. 'He wanted to know everything about him, what sort of man he was, what he liked to do, the sports he liked to play. I was able to tell him everything, how his grandfather had been a wonderful man and a loyal friend.' William also told Mohamed he knew his mother had suffered at the hands of his other grandfather, Prince Philip. 'He said it had been going on for years, ever since the separation, and he thanked me for the help and support I had given his mother through all her troubles. He was remarkably mature for a teenager. He didn't shout or even sound angry. He was just very sad and disappointed. There was a lot of his mother in that boy then.

You could see the streak of independence that she always showed and even then I could tell he was going to be a very strong character in years to come. Much stronger than his father. After all, what kind of man can he be to give up someone like Diana for a woman like Camilla?'

It has been suggested that, since the death of his mother, William has come to be more and more under the influence of the Windsor/Mountbattens, in particular his grandfather, Prince Philip, who is recognized as the most aggressive and, at times, unpleasant member of the Royal Family. Mohamed Al Fayed does not think this will have a lasting effect on the character of the young prince. 'I got to know William very well when he stayed with me and I could see how strong he was even then. I don't believe there is any chance that he will adopt any of the less likeable aspects of Philip's character. The one thing I think he is missing, and will continue to miss, is a family life. He saw how happy my family were together and he loved it. He's not going to get the same togetherness from the Royals. They don't really know what family life is all about.'

Mr Al Fayed may be perfectly sincere in his feelings about William and Prince Philip; there's no reason to suppose otherwise. But the facts are that William and his paternal grandfather are extremely close. They share many of the same interests, enjoy each other's company and even when William and Harry were small, Philip would spend hours playing with them. The image of him allowing young children to crawl all over him, messing up his clothes and persuading him to make up stories to tell them, is very much at odds with what most people imagine. The more popular impression of Philip is as a crusty, bad-tempered and impatient old man. William has always got along brilliantly with him and it was Philip who taught him to shoot and with whom he spends days in the gorse at Balmoral when they are stalking deer.

Prince Philip is also able to answer many of the questions that William feels he cannot ask his father: such as does he regret having had to relinquish his naval career when he married and does he think William would make a good soldier. Philip is also sympathetic when it comes to William and girls, being a firm believer in playing the field before you settle down. Their relationship is based on solid friendship and each knows he can say anything he wants to the other. It has also been suggested that Philip sees more of himself in William than he does in his own sons. There is a toughness there that is lacking in them and he believes it must come from his genes.

One of the biggest problems William has to face is that his mother was the most famous woman in the world. Mohamed Al Fayed's son Dodi also grew up in the shadow of a famous father who could give him anything money could buy, but, as Mohamed explains, William's situation is not the same:

> Yes, but there's a big difference. It's true that my Dodi had a lot of advantages to begin with, but he made his own way, producing an Oscar-winning film, *Chariots of Fire*, so he never found having me as a father to be a problem. He was successful in his own right. William is going to be King one day, just through an accident of birth. It's not his fault and I don't think he would choose it if he were allowed to make a choice. After all, he wants to be normal like everybody else. He wants to go to the pub, go dancing, have girlfriends, live his own life. But he can't. There's always someone controlling him and trying to manipulate him like a robot. And then there's this constant attention by the press. It can't be easy for him to have anything like a normal life. In fact the only time he has been able to do it was when he was staying with me. We didn't treat him like he was different from any of our own children and he liked that. It was the first and only time he could behave like a normal teenager.

Mr Al Fayed even went to the trouble of hosting a private party at one of St Tropez's most fashionable discos so that William and Harry could enjoy themselves without any intrusion from outsiders.

Does Mohamed believe his son and Diana would have married, and if so, would he have welcomed her and her children into his family? 'They were very serious, on the brink of getting engaged, and Dodi, William and Harry got on famously. They shared many of the same interests: water sports, football and cars. If you could have seen William and Dodi together it was wonderful. Dodi was just like an older brother. I would have been delighted and very proud to have been the boys' step-grandfather and the rest of my family would have welcomed them with open arms.'

Mohamed Al Fayed is a man of enormous personal wealth, one of the few people in the world who was able to give Diana and her boys the sort of privacy and security they demanded on holiday. But although she was a princess and they were Royal Highnesses, it did not follow that there was a great deal of formality when they were around. Mohamed reveals:

Both Princess Diana and William loved water sports and liked nothing better than sharing a jet ski, as they did on this occasion in St Tropez in the South of France.

There was none at all. They did whatever they wanted to do. They were all early risers, even on vacation, and they spent most of the day in swimsuits, either on the jet skis, which they loved, sailing or going out on the yacht [the *Jonikal*]. There was no difference between them and my family. I didn't treat them any differently and they didn't expect anything special. I think it was the first time any of them had seen a normal family like ours. It doesn't matter what we've got, we are still down to earth. There's no protocol, no restrictions, we are all totally relaxed with each other and William and his mother and brother enjoyed our company as much as we enjoyed theirs. I don't think they had ever experienced anything like it before – or since.

When the boys and Diana returned to Britain after their holiday in the South of France in 1997, they each wrote thanking Mohamed for his hospitality. William's letter said: '. . . The *Jonikal* was an amazing piece of kit and I loved sailing on it. . . . I can't thank you enough for a superb holiday and I'm now very much looking forward to using my Harrods Card!' Diana also wrote saying how much she had

William and Harry both wanted Mohamed Al Fayed to attend the funeral of their mother and they were pleased when they saw him in the congregation at Westminster Abbey, still in mourning for his son, Dodi, who had been buried some days earlier.

enjoyed the holiday and how much she was looking forward to the next time, which in her case was only a few weeks away, and it was during that final holiday that the fatal car crash occurred. But, of course, from the tone of her letter there was no hint that anything tragic was to take place within weeks. She thanked Mohamed for his '. . . kindness, generosity and patience . . .' adding '. . . You gave the three of us a great deal of happiness and a holiday to remember.' It was to be the last holiday they would spend together.

If there is one regret that Mohamed Al Fayed has about his relationship with Prince William and Prince Harry it is that since the death of their mother there has been no contact.

I'm sure they would like to get in touch with me and of course I would love to see them again. But I understand how difficult it must be, particularly for William, to keep up an old friendship with someone who was close to his beloved mother when the rest of the Royal Family are trying to cut her from their memories. William is an independent young man with a wonderful personality, who will one day be a brilliant King – if the monarchy survives when his time comes. I think he will be one of the best. He won't be controlled. He will be loving and popular. . . . My door is always open to him and his brother.'

three
Diana's
Funeral

The day of Diana's funeral was obviously the saddest but also the most traumatic William would ever have to face. Not only was he about to say a final goodbye to his mother, but he would be required to conduct himself with the self-control the Royal Family prides itself on during this most public of private moments. At the vulnerable age of fifteen, he had decided, along with his even younger brother, Harry, that he would walk behind their mother's coffin on the sad journey to Westminster Abbey. He knew the eyes of the world would be upon him, and his father had allowed him to make the final choice as to whether he would take part in the procession or not. There was never really any question that he would not. William and Harry were determined to show their public support and love for their mother on her final journey. But neither of them could have imagined the extent of the public emotion that threatened to overwhelm them during that final journey. Prince Charles was to say later, 'I have never been more proud of my sons.'

In an interview given to the *Guardian* five years later – significantly, just before Althorp was due to open for its summer season – Diana's brother, Charles, the 9th Earl Spencer, claimed he was misled into believing that his Royal nephews wanted to accompany their mother's coffin. 'I was told they wanted to do it and they would like it if I were there; I now know that's not true,' he said, without elaborating on how he knew. Earl Spencer stated that he believed that Buckingham Palace officials wanted him, William and Harry to walk behind the

The Prince of Wales looks reassuringly at his sons as they stand outside Westminster Abbey with Earl Spencer after the funeral of Diana, Princess of Wales. For William and Harry this was not only the saddest but also the most traumatic day of their young lives.

coffin on its journey to Westminster Abbey, saying that was the only reason he agreed to take part himself as his own feelings were that it would be far too painful for the young princes. The Palace has never commented officially on the subject, or on Earl Spencer's remarks, but there is little doubt that Prince Charles had consulted The Queen and together they had decided to allow William and Harry to make the decision for themselves.

When on 31 August 1997 Diana died so tragically in a car crash in a Paris underpass, in a vehicle driven by an employee of Dodi Fayed, who was also killed, her children were asleep in bed at Balmoral. Initially there was confusion about the true circumstances of the accident, with first reports suggesting that Diana had merely been injured. Prince Charles's request for an aircraft of the Queen's Flight to go to her side was turned down by The Queen's private secretary on the grounds that 'only the Sovereign can authorize such transport'. Consequently it was decided not to alert the boys immediately.

Even when the facts of her death had been confirmed – and Charles had been granted permission to have an official aircraft to bring her body back to Britain later – William and Harry were not woken. The Queen and Prince Charles felt there was little to be gained in disturbing them in the early hours of the morning. They were right. There was nothing they could do that could not wait a short time, so it was the senior members of the family who stayed up for the rest of the night talking about the implications of the death of this 'semi-detached' member of the family. But none of them had the slightest notion of the impact it would have, or the sense of national dismay and bewilderment that would follow, or the lasting effect on the Royal Family.

It was Prince Charles who broke the news to his sons in William's bedroom the following morning, with his arms around them. When Charles asked Harry to join him in his brother's room, they both suspected that something was wrong, but neither, of course, had an inkling of the magnitude of the news he was to give them. They were very quiet and controlled, and even though their parents had been divorced for some time, it was the boys who comforted their father, rather than the other way around. Always an emotional man, Charles broke down when he had to tell them the saddest news any parent can give his children. Later that day the three Waleses walked together in the grounds at Balmoral, chatting about their memories of Diana. Neither The Queen nor Prince Philip interfered; they were there if they were needed but this was a time when father and sons wanted to be alone and they respected their wishes.

The Queen was naturally sympathetic to her grandsons, but she made one huge mistake – or at least her advisers did – which was not to insist that Diana be included in the prayers that are traditionally offered for the Royal Family when she and Prince Philip attended morning service at Crathie parish church on Sunday morning. Ever since the divorce Diana's name had been dropped from the list of Royals for whom prayers were said, but it had been expected that on this occasion she would be mentioned. Not a word was spoken. The Queen was blamed for apparently showing such lack of compassion towards her

William and Harry joined the Prince of Wales to look at the carpet of floral tributes left at Kensington Palace in the days following the death of Diana, Princess of Wales. William said later that he knew his mother was loved but, until then, didn't realize how much.

former daughter-in-law. Prince William was desperately upset. He had expected prayers to be offered for his mother and could not understand the omission. What happened was that the minister at Crathie church had not been given any instructions from Balmoral regarding Diana, so assumed that he should just carry on as normal. In the confusion The Queen's private secretary had not thought to say anything, nor had her equerry and neither, apparently, had Prince Philip. It was a combination of errors that resulted in a blast of criticism directed straight at The Queen.

Later the grandparents would show the support their son and grandsons were going to need. It was The Queen's decision that William and Harry should remain at Balmoral for the time being and she was proved to be right. The scenes of mass hysteria in London would have been unbearable, and in the days before they returned to the capital the two youngsters were protected from the media and the public until they were ready to face the crowds that had gathered.

When William and Harry did arrive in London they saw the thousands of bouquets of flowers that had been placed at the gates of Buckingham Palace and Kensington Palace and witnessed the lines of people waiting for up to twelve hours to sign the books of condolence at St James's Palace. As the thousands of mourners patiently queued to pay their respects, Mohamed Al Fayed was given permission to send along his distinctive Harrods green vans to provide refreshments. It was a practical and very welcome gesture on his part.

On the Friday before the funeral, Charles, accompanied by William and Harry, joined those outside Kensington Palace who were still leaving bunches of flowers. They stopped and talked to many of the people who had congregated there. William thanked everyone he spoke to for their tributes to his mother and for their condolences. He later told a friend that the multi-coloured carpet of flowers was the most moving sight he had ever seen, adding, 'I knew my mother was loved but I had no idea how much and by how many.' One of the women who was about the same age as Diana, remarked, 'To see the boys like this breaks my heart. But I am so proud of them and I know their mother would have been.' And when The Queen and Philip arrived back at Buckingham Palace, they made an unscheduled stop outside the gates and both got out, mingling with the mourners. Philip in particular chatted with the onlookers, taking bouquets from their hands and placing them in front of the Palace railings.

William pauses to read some of the tributes to his late mother that had been placed at the gates of Kensington Palace. He was deeply moved by some of the comments and told onlookers how touched he was by their messages of sympathy.

In the days between Diana's death and her funeral, William watched with increasing fascination as the story of her life was unfolded time and time again on every television channel. The marriage and its break-up were discussed endlessly by 'experts' and 'close friends' and later William said he had learned more about his mother in that week than he had in the previous sixteen years. Foremost among the criticisms voiced both in Britain and abroad was that the Royals were not attuned to the desires of the people, who wanted The Queen and her family openly to share their grief and for the 'people's princess' to be given a suitable funeral. It would turn out to be a spectacular display of Royal pageantry, even if it had all been arranged at the last minute.

On 6 September 1997, a brilliantly sunny and clear autumn day in London, the coffin containing the body of Diana, Princess of Wales was carried on a gun-carriage from Kensington Palace to Westminster Abbey where a 2,000-strong congregation included leading politicians, show-business celebrities, personal friends and representatives of the many organizations she had helped.

William was particularly pleased that the people involved in his mother's favourite charities had been invited to walk in the procession and take part in the funeral service in the Abbey. He knew that she would not have wished the

All the Royal Family attended the funeral of Diana, Princess of Wales, even the 97-year-old Queen Mother, seen here with The Queen at the entrance to Westminster Abbey.

occasion to be taken over by the ranks of politicians, statesmen and foreign emissaries who normally have pride of place at such events. He also wanted, and was relieved to find, that many of her personal friends had received invitations and were seated in prominent positions.

On the route to Westminster Abbey, the cortège passed the gates of Buckingham Palace where a group of Royals led by The Queen waited. As Diana's coffin drew level The Queen was seen to bow her head, quickly followed by the rest of the party. It was totally unexpected and was reported as an unprecedented and spontaneous gesture contained in no book of Royal protocol. But The Queen got it exactly right. It was the correct thing to do at the time and demonstrated that she recognized the affection and respect the people had for Diana even if the Royal Family themselves had shown little love for her in the latter years of her life.

Prince William and his brother Harry, together with Prince Charles, Prince Philip and Earl Spencer, Diana's brother, joined the procession as it passed St James's Palace and walked in silence behind the coffin the rest of the way to the Abbey. The only sound that could be heard from the watching tens of thousands lining the route was that of gentle sobbing and the most poignant element of the ceremonial was the sight of a simple wreath of white roses on the coffin bearing the one word 'Mummy'.

Luciano Pavarotti, who attended, had been asked to sing at the service of his friend but said he was too distressed to perform. Sir Elton John played and sang a special version of his song 'Candle in the Wind', which was written originally for Marilyn Monroe, even though he too was grief-stricken and said later that the only way he managed to get through the ordeal was to '. . . close my eyes and grit my teeth'. William was pleased that Sir Elton had been asked to sing this song, as it had been one of his mother's favourites. Mohamed Al Fayed had been invited to attend the funeral service and he arrived still in mourning for his son, who had been buried earlier. He later told me that he received a letter of condolence from The Queen but not one word from any other member of the Royal Family.

Prince Charles left the decision to his sons about whether they would walk behind their mother's coffin in her funeral procession. They agreed they would walk and were joined by their grandfather, the Duke of Edinburgh, and their uncle, Earl Spencer.

William and Harry watched as, with a mixture of military pomp, great passion and deep sadness, their mother was laid to rest in what was described as a 'unique funeral' for a unique person. This was Buckingham Palace's excuse for not allowing the occasion to be a State or Semi-State Funeral. As Diana was no longer a Royal Highness or a member of the Royal Family she was not entitled to anything approaching an official funeral, but the Palace realized that the people would not tolerate anything less for the woman they adored, and Prince Charles insisted, over several objections from other members of his family and senior courtiers, that his former wife should be buried with all the dignity and ceremonial he felt she deserved. It was estimated that a worldwide television audience of over 2 billion watched the proceedings live – more even than had viewed the wedding of Charles and Diana in 1981. It was the largest audience in television history.

The Very Reverend Dr Wesley Carr greeted the funeral cortège at Westminster Abbey and in his opening remarks summed up perfectly the feelings of those present and elsewhere when he said 'Diana profoundly influenced this nation and the world. . . . She was someone for whom, from afar, we dared to feel affection.'

During the funeral service Earl Spencer delivered an eloquent if somewhat 'holier than thou' eulogy to his sister in which he described himself and others of the Spencer clan as the young princes' 'blood family', conveniently ignoring the fact that they already had a father. It was a direct challenge to Prince Charles and the Royal Family and although it was applauded by many in the Abbey and by the crowds listening outside on a public address system, an equal number felt the speech inappropriate and a deliberate insult. Charles Spencer later said '. . . it wasn't a general criticism of the Royal Family. It was aimed very directly.' However, five years later it was revealed, at the trial of Princess Diana's former butler, Paul Burrell, on charges of stealing 300 items belonging to her, that Spencer had refused his sister's request for a house on his estate because it would be 'inconvenient' for his own family.

Opposite: *The funeral of Diana, Princess of Wales, was a mixture of pageantry, pomp and personal sadness. As the party of Welsh guardsmen carried her coffin with perfect military precision down the aisle in Westminster Abbey the only sounds were of gentle sobbing.*

There has not been evidence of any particular closeness between Earl Spencer and his nephews since the day of the funeral, apart from when William visited his mother's grave on the anniversary of her fortieth birthday, and neither brother has expressed a view – at least publicly – about their feelings when their uncle spoke. Prince Charles took it as a personal attack on himself, both as a former husband and as a parent, and has never forgiven Spencer. There is also a coolness between him and Diana's two sisters, Sarah and Jane, the latter of whom is married to Lord (Robert) Fellowes, formerly The Queen's private secretary and the man who Diana blamed, unjustly, for many of her troubles with the Royal Family. So these days none of William and Harry's Spencer aunts and uncles has any real contact with their Royal nephews in spite of the fact that William had always enjoyed a warm relationship with both Sarah and Jane.

Earl Spencer admits 'I haven't seen William for a while,' adding 'I have seen Harry very regularly. There are also text messages, e-mails – there are all sorts of communication rather than just physical contact and there's nothing I wouldn't do for them.' Then he adds a curious point saying, 'I've seen the Prime Minister about their privacy', which is unusual and presumably unnecessary as their privacy and security is the responsibility of the Royalty Protection Department. Referring back to his speech in Westminster Abbey, Earl Spencer denies that he was challenging the Royal Family's role in bringing up William and Harry. 'I was just there to protect them and give them a different direction if they needed it. . . . What I can say is that they may not be encouraged to stay in touch with their mother's side of the family.' His anger is very obviously still directed at Prince Charles, to whom he spoke only once in the five years following Diana's death, and that was only because they happened to be guests at the same function in South Africa.

It was the Spencer family – Diana's mother, brother and two sisters – who decided that she should be buried at Althorp, and the Royal Family were pleased – and relieved – to agree as it removed a further problem for them. If Diana had not been buried at her family's home, The Queen and Prince Charles would have had to make provision at one of the Royal burial grounds. As she was no longer a member of the family, and not, technically, still a royal, this would have caused all sorts of difficulties. The Royal Family are not very adept at facing situations for which there are no precedents.

Prince William

William displayed a truly Royal self-control during the funeral of his mother and exhibited a maturity far beyond his years under the gaze of thousands of people lining the route and millions more watching on television.

For William, the funeral was the climax of several years of upheaval, caused first of all by the separation and divorce of his parents, the rancour that followed between Diana and Charles and the rest of the Royal Family and then the furore over the much-publicized love affair of his father and Camilla Parker Bowles. William, who had been only eleven years old when his parents separated, hated the publicity that surrounded the divorce and he fully believed his mother when she later told him that neither she nor his father had wanted the final break-up mainly because of the public humiliation they felt their sons might suffer. As it happened there was no 'fall-out' in the aftermath of the divorce and at school the boys found themselves to be part of a large minority, for many of their fellow pupils had divorced parents. Diana said The Queen, urged on by Prince Philip, had forced the divorce on them in spite of their own willingness to continue their marriage but lead separate lives.

It would have been perfectly understandable if William had decided to retreat into himself, and he did show signs of being introverted for a while after the divorce, but this lasted for only a short time and within weeks he was his old self. The constant interruptions to his otherwise normal way of life, his education at a time when he was studying for examinations and his training for eventual kingship, would have been excuse enough for him to claim he could not continue. The death of his mother and the manner of it was the ultimate tragedy. He does not appear to have been permanently damaged by those events, but that is only to judge by outward appearances. Only he knows the truth. His mother was a flawed character who suffered enormous damage at the hands of the Royal Family after her separation from Charles, and the constant tug-of-love that existed between them, with their children in the middle, must have left an indelible mark on the two boys who were then at their most impressionable age.

In the final years of her life, Diana often went to William with her problems, placing a weight on his young shoulders no teenager should have to bear. She asked his advice when she was told that as part of her divorce settlement, she would have to lose her right to be called Her Royal Highness. Diana later said it was not because she was going to miss it (though others close to her said this was not the case) but because of the effect it might have on her sons. William told her not to worry about such trivialities, adding, 'You'll still be Mummy.' It was exactly what she wanted to hear and showed great percipience on his part, even at the tender age of fifteen.

Since the death of Diana there has been endless speculation about her legacy to the nation. Is it the way in which she made public awareness of such hitherto unmentionable diseases as AIDS more acceptable or her participation in the campaign to remove land-mines? In point of fact her true legacy is her son William. He is a constant reminder to the nation – and to the Royal Family – of the future of the monarchy and that it appears to be safe for at least the next two generations.

four
A Royal
Birth

Prince William Arthur Philip Louis of Wales was born at 9.03 p.m. on 21 June 1982 and weighed in at a healthy 7 lb 1½ oz. He made history at the moment of his birth by being the first heir presumptive to the throne not to be born in a castle, palace or other Royal residence, but in an ordinary hospital. Not that he was the first Royal baby to be born in hospital, both of Princess Anne's children, Peter and Zara Phillips, had been born at the same hospital as had the children of the Duke and Duchess of Gloucester and the son and daughter of Prince and Princess Michael of Kent.

It was Princess Diana, encouraged by the Royal gynaecologist George Pinker, who persuaded a reluctant Prince Charles to agree that the birth should take place in the private Lindo Wing of St Mary's in Paddington. Here every modern item of medical equipment was to hand, but the rooms, even at £100 a night – expensive for those days – were far from luxurious, even spartan. As it turned out, the decision to have the baby in hospital was the right one as Diana endured a sixteen-hour labour, so would probably have been moved to hospital from the Palace in any case. The change was popular and welcomed by the media – as there was more access and they would have the opportunity of seeing her and the child earlier than if they had been protected behind the walls of Kensington Palace – and also by young mothers everywhere. It was a sign that William was going to be brought into a world far different from that his father had joined in 1948.

| NHS Number | LSBSS 115 | **BIRTH** | | Entry No. | **115** |

Registration district Westminster
Sub-district Westminster
Administrative area City of Westminster

CHILD

1. Date and place of birth — Twenty first June 1982 St Mary's Hospital Praed Street Westminster

2. Name and surname — His Royal Highness Prince William Arthur Philip Louis

3. Sex — Male

FATHER

4. Name and surname — His Royal Highness Prince Charles Philip Arthur George Prince of Wales

5. Place of birth — Westminster

6. Occupation — Prince of the United Kingdom

MOTHER

7. Name and surname — Her Royal Highness The Princess of Wales

8. Place of birth — Sandringham Norfolk

9.(a) Maiden surname — SPENCER

(b) Surname at marriage if different from maiden surname — —

10. Usual address (if different from place of child's birth) — Highgrove Near Tetbury Gloucestershire

INFORMANT

11. Name and surname (if not the mother or father) — —

12. Qualification — Father

13. Usual address (if different from that in 10 above) — —

14. I certify that the particulars entered above are true to the best of my knowledge and belief

Charles .... Signature of informant

15. Date of registration — Nineteenth July 1982

16. Signature of registrar — Joan V. Webb Registrar

17. Name given after registration, and surname —

Prince William's birth certificate. He was registered by his father, who gave his occupation as 'Prince of the United Kingdom' at Westminster on 19 July 1982.

Prince Charles had remained with his wife throughout the labour and birth and as soon as he knew everything was all right, he telephoned The Queen at Buckingham Palace to tell her she had another grandson. Within two hours, all the immediate members of the family were informed, first the Queen Mother at Clarence House, then Prince Philip, who was dining at Cambridge, and who downed a large brandy when he heard the news. Princess Anne, on tour in the USA, gave a short, sharp reply to reporters when she was asked for her reaction to the birth. But the reason was that she had not been told officially and was not prepared to give an off-the-cuff quote that might rebound. Later, when she had been told by Buckingham Palace, she expressed her pleasure in the warmest terms. Prince Andrew, still serving in the Falklands, and Prince Edward, at Gordonstoun, also received the news within minutes of the birth. Princess Margaret was at the theatre when an announcement was made from the stage by the dancer Wayne Sleep – who would later delight audiences by dancing on stage with Diana – and Earl Spencer, Diana's father, received a personal telephone call from Prince Charles. He said he was 'over the moon'. Diana's mother, Frances Shand Kydd, was also in London and when she was told she rang her mother, Ruth, Lady Fermoy, one of the Queen Mother's ladies-in-waiting, who passed on the good news to Diana's sisters Sarah and Jane and her brother Charles, still at Eton.

An official announcement was posted on the gates of Buckingham Palace where crowds had gathered, as they always do on special Royal occasions. The Prime Minister was informed and the Palace machinery moved smoothly into action to tell the heads of Government of all Commonwealth countries. Hundreds of people had waited outside the hospital to hear the announcement of the birth and they were thrilled when Prince Charles said: 'The birth of our son has given us both more pleasure than you can imagine. It has made me incredibly proud and somewhat amazed.'

The crowds of onlookers, reporters, photographers and television crews did not have long to wait for their first glimpse of the future King as Diana decided to leave St Mary's within thirty-six hours of giving birth. Prince Charles carried his as yet unnamed son – the nurses had fastened a band around his tiny wrist on which they had written the legend 'Baby Wales' – out on to the steps of the hospital where he was subjected to his first official photo-call before being driven to Kensington Palace, his home for the next sixteen years.

Diana always claimed this was her favourite maternity dress and she wore it to show off her new-born baby, unnamed at this point, when she and Prince Charles brought him home to Kensington Palace for the first time.

Diana had never doubted that she was destined to be a mother. She said it was her natural role in life and some years later, speaking about her children, she said, 'They mean everything to me. I always give them love and affection.' She also gave William his nickname of 'Wills', which was not entirely approved of by the rest of the Royal Family who do not care for diminutives. Nobody could imagine Prince Charles being called 'Charlie', least of all himself.

When Prince William was christened at Buckingham Palace in August 1982 he behaved 'impeccably' throughout the ceremony, but 'howled' afterwards. His mother found the perfect remedy – her little finger.

Princess Diana revealed that William would not wear the usual old-fashioned nappies made of towelling that Royal babies had traditionally worn – as had most babies until a few years earlier – but more hygienic, disposable ones like every other modern mother insisted on using. And as with all other aspects of Royal life, this too was the subject of much discussion. One of William's former nannies recalled that Prince Charles could not see any reason for a change; just as some years later he did not see why his son should go to nursery school when he himself had received his early education at home. But Diana won – on both occasions.

There was intense interest in the child from the moment he was born and in those first few days increasing speculation about what he was to be called. Diana favoured one of the more modern, fashionable names of the day, but she lost out to Charles and The Queen who insisted that he had to have a traditional Royal name as befitted a future sovereign. They were not particularly concerned about his secondary names – as long as the initials did not make an acronym that would cause derision – but they were insistent that the name by which he would be known was one that had been used by Royalty for generations. William was the

Right: *King Constantine of the Hellenes is one of the Royal Family's closest friends. A resident of London for many years, His Majesty is godfather to William and takes his responsibilities very seriously.*

Opposite: *The Duchess of Westminster – known as 'Tally' – is William's godmother. She was the personal choice of both Diana and Charles and has remained close to both William and Harry. Here she is seen with her husband the Duke of Westminster, said to be Britain's richest landowner.*

perfect choice, going back a thousand years to William the Conqueror, even if Diana chose to call him by the affectionate abbreviation 'Wills' right from the start. Later she added another nickname, 'Wombat', which she often used when writing to him at school.

William was christened on 4 August 1982 (his great-grandmother's birthday) in the Music Room at Buckingham Palace and in the choice of godparents his mother had to give way to Prince Charles and The Queen, apart from one godmother. She was the 24-year-old Duchess of Westminster, Natalia, known as 'Tally'. Not only was she the personal choice of Princess Diana, as one of her closest friends, but her own mother, Lady 'Gina' Kennard, had known The Queen since childhood and was one of her oldest friends, while her grandparents, Sir Harold and Lady Zia Wernher, had been long-standing companions of The Queen and Prince Philip since their marriage in 1947. The Duchess could also trace her family line back to the Russian Royal Family, so 'Tally' Westminster was a happy choice all round. Speaking about being a godmother, she said:

I had known both Prince Charles and Diana for many years. Nevertheless the invitation came as a complete surprise and I was, of course, delighted and honoured. One of my children is the same age as William and when we used to come down to London from our home in Cheshire, we would often join

Diana and William in the nursery at Kensington Palace for tea. It was a very domestic scene and totally informal. William and Harry still come to stay with us from time to time and they are great fun, there's no stuffiness about either of them. They are always completely at ease. Of course William loves to shoot and he is an excellent shot so he likes coming to us and we love having him.

The Royal godparents were King Constantine of the Hellenes, who was to become a great favourite of Diana's, and Princess Alexandra, with Countess Mountbatten's eldest son, Norton, Lord Romsey, another cousin and member of the Royal 'inner circle'. Lady Susan Hussey, one of The Queen's longest-serving ladies-in-waiting, was delighted to be asked to be a godmother and Prince Charles completed the line-up by inviting his mentor, Sir Laurens van der Post. This last was a purely symbolic gesture as godparents are, in theory, supposed to make sure that the child they are sponsoring has spiritual guidance until they reach the age of majority. As Sir Laurens was already seventy-four

Almost a year old and Prince William is fascinated by the camera as he is cuddled by his parents at their apartment in Kensington Palace.

when the christening took place, it was highly unlikely that he was going to be able to perform this function for the full term and as it happened he died long before William reached his twenty-first birthday.

The Archbishop of Canterbury, Dr (later Lord) Robert Runcie officiated at the ceremony and by all accounts the baby behaved beautifully during the ceremony but howled afterwards. The Lily Font, used for every Royal christening since 1840 when Queen Victoria's eldest child, Princess Victoria, was baptised, was brought out, and the baby wore the same Honiton lace christening gown, first worn by Victoria's second child and first son, the future King Edward VII, in 1842. Afterwards, a lunch party for sixty guests – small by Royal standards – was held in the Palace's State Dining Room, with the christening cake, by tradition, being the top layer of the Prince and Princess of Wales's wedding cake. The Surgeon Gynaecologist to The Queen, Mr George Pinker, who was later knighted by Her Majesty, was a guest, along with the four nurses who had looked after the baby in St Mary's Hospital.

William was second in the line of succession to the throne and genealogists were quick to emphasize that he was very much an English prince, more so than his father, who shared Prince Philip's foreign blood. William was said to be the most English member of the Royal Family since Elizabeth I with 39 per cent of his blood being pure English, the remainder spread between Ireland, Scotland, the USA and Germany. Apparently there is no Welsh blood in Prince William of Wales.

Diana was determined that she would be a hands-on mother, and to be fair, Prince Charles also decided he would attempt to be a modern father. He had, after all, been present at the birth of his son, though he later admitted it was not the most pleasant event he had attended. In fact he remarked that it was a humbling experience, which he found '. . . rather a shock to my system'. But he added, diplomatically, 'I think it is a very good thing for a husband to be with a mother when she is expecting a baby.'

At Kensington Palace there was, of course, a nanny to take care of all the day-to-day chores, but both Diana and Charles liked to see William being bathed and fed whenever they could. Diana even changed nappies on occasion; Charles drew the line at this point. His father, Prince Philip, who has always been a great favourite with young children, saw no reason to involve himself in the domestic life of his own children when they were infants and did not see why

Above left: *Prince Charles handles his new baby son very carefully as he carries him in his Moses basket down the steps of the aircraft of The Queen's Flight as they arrive at Aberdeen Airport en route to Balmoral for their summer holiday in August 1982. The Prince was later criticized for not placing William in a special child's car seat for the rest of the journey by road.*

Above right: *Nanny Barbara Barnes carrying Prince William off the Royal Flight as they arrive in Alice Springs, Australia, in March 1983 at the start of a six-week tour of the Antipodes. Diana had refused to be parted from William and so this was the first time a Royal baby had been taken on an official overseas tour.*

Opposite: *Diana made sure William did not wear shoes while he was still an infant so that his feet could develop naturally. Here he is obviously capable of standing up – but needs the helping hands of Mummy.*

Charles should do so. But he did not interfere, even if, privately, he thought it was taking parenting a little too far.

Prince Charles was seen carrying William in a Moses basket down the steps of an aircraft of the Queen's Flight when they arrived in Scotland, another Royal first, but when the baby was placed in a car still in his basket, Charles was criticized for not making sure that a proper child car seat was used.

The Queen recognized some of the problems that were going to face her daughter-in-law: trying to be a modern mother and, at the same time, having to accompany her husband on the never-ending round of public duties. Within weeks of William's birth came the first big test when Prince Charles and Diana were scheduled to leave Britain for an extended tour of Australia. The Queen and the late Queen Mother both felt that the baby should be left at home to be looked after by his nanny, supervised by them. Diana was having none of it. She was determined that if she was going, so was William, and she got her way. The photographs of nanny Barbara Barnes carrying William down the steps of the aircraft as they landed on Australian soil were seen around the world, and

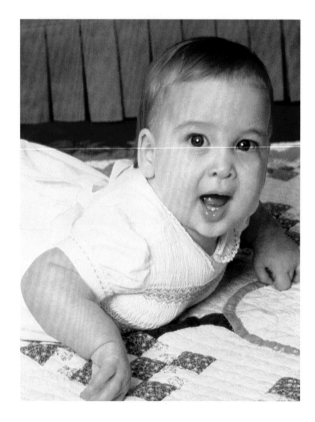

William loved to crawl – as most babies do – and the nursery at Kensington Palace was the ideal place to practise.

William's second birthday, 21 June 1984. This photograph was taken in the gardens of Kensington Palace.

there was general approval of the fact that this young Royal mother had decided not to leave her baby behind.

From infancy, William's nanny played a vital role in his life. It has always been the same with all the Royals. They see their parents a couple of times a day – washed and polished – and for the rest of their time are looked after by servants, who then become very important, at least for the time they are employed. William's nanny used to take him for walks in Kensington Gardens with an armed bodyguard keeping a watchful eye from a discreet distance. They would often meet other nannies or mothers pushing their babies and stop to chat and rarely did any of them know whom they were talking to. Those who did cotton on, never disclosed the fact that they had met the newest member of the Royal Family, even when, on occasion, they also met one of the other residents of Kensington Palace stopping to look in on the baby. Princess Alice, Duchess of Gloucester, at the time of writing the oldest living member of the family, loved to walk in the Gardens and she always enjoyed chatting to William's nanny about the progress of the baby.

The strict order of precedence within the Royal Family was maintained even among its youngest members. When William was still a babe in arms he would occupy pride of place over all the other infants whenever they were introduced into The Queen's presence. The nannies would line up with William first, followed by his cousins, the children of the Dukes of Gloucester and Kent, with those of Prince and Princess Michael of Kent bringing up the rear. And when he was old enough to understand what was going on, William quickly realized how important it was to maintain his prime position in his generation of Royal children. On one occasion, Harry jumped the queue, to be hauled rapidly back by his older brother and told to 'remember who comes first'.

In the early years, William was thoroughly spoilt and during a visit to Balmoral when he was barely fifteen months old pressed an alarm button that alerted the police in the nearby town of Ballater. His nanny was blamed for allowing her young charge to disrupt the tranquillity of The Queen's Highland home, but Charles and Diana considered it merely a childish prank. The trouble in those early days was that both Diana and Nanny Barnes doted on William and could see no wrong in anything he did. Prince Charles was equally loving, but having been brought up in a less relaxed atmosphere by his own nannies and nursemaids – in an age when children were expected to be seen and not heard – felt the boy needed some sort of discipline to curb his natural high spirits.

Matters came to a head shortly after the birth of Harry, when William began treating the servants in the household without the respect and good manners they were entitled to expect. Prince Charles had always, from childhood, been taught that politeness and consideration should be shown to everyone, including his parent's domestic servants, and he refused to accept Diana's explanation that William's behaviour was just exuberance and all a normal part of growing up. At three years old, William suddenly found himself being smacked when he was naughty, and he also got the occasional tap from one of the servants at Kensington Palace – when neither his nanny nor one of his parents were looking. One of the reasons for the difficulty was that William was the centre of his mother's life. In her eyes he could do no wrong. But Diana eventually agreed that he needed to learn how to behave with children of his own age and that the first stage of his education should begin.

five
Early
Days

In deciding how William's education should start, there was, however, one big problem. If Prince Charles had had his way, William would not have gone to school until he was seven or eight years old. He felt there was no good reason why his son should not follow the path he and his brothers had taken and receive his early education at home with a governess to give him private lessons. That may have been all well and good in 1951, but some thirty-odd years on Diana realized that her son should come to terms with meeting other children, and get away from the 'hothouse' atmosphere of palaces and castles, and she persuaded Charles to allow William to attend nursery school. This was no simple matter. Many people, including The Queen, had to be consulted before such a momentous decision could be agreed. Preliminary visits were made to a number of suitable establishments in the area; friends of the couple were asked their opinion of the various places; the routes between Kensington Palace and the potential schools were examined and the Royalty Protection Department carried out security checks at all of them before Charles and Diana decided on Mrs Mynor's Nursery School in Nottinghill Gate. This could be reached in minutes by driving from the Palace up through the private Kensington Palace gardens – said to be the most secure avenue in Britain.

Before William started at the nursery school, his mother wrote or spoke to every other parent to apologize in advance if William's presence disrupted their children's daily routine. Prince Charles's office also asked all the national

William's first day at nursery school in September 1983, and as he leaves to go home he proudly shows off the finger mouse he had made for his mother.

Opposite: *The boys liked nothing better than dressing up in uniforms. Here they are enjoying being firemen for the day, climbing over the engine watched by Princess Diana in January 1988.*

newspaper editors to give William a little breathing space when he began his education. Nevertheless, on his first day (24 September 1985) no fewer than 150 reporters and photographers were waiting outside Mrs Mynor's Nursery School. It did not seem to upset the three-year-old in the slightest. He had not then learned to hate the media as he later did.

William was the only child in the school to have an armed bodyguard with him, the school was equipped with a 'panic button' connected to the nearest police station in case of intruders, and William's classroom was fitted with special bullet-proof glass. For the first term he only attended on two mornings a week, then later it was every day.

But the transition from being the centre of attention at Kensington Palace to being just one of the children at nursery school was not easy. William, having been thoroughly spoilt by his nanny and his mother, thought he could continue his bad behaviour with his fellow pupils, seeing no reason to restrain himself just because he was in a class of twenty. He was involved in several fights in the playground and on more than one occasion his police bodyguard had to intervene. Part of the trouble was that when he arrived home after school, he would tell his mother his version of the story and she would invariably take his

side, cuddling and kissing him, thereby ruining the efforts of those in charge of him at nursery during the day. But even Diana eventually realized that William's behaviour was getting out of hand, and she blamed everyone but herself, the principal culprit – in her eyes – being Barbara Barnes. It was very convenient to blame Barbara; as a servant she could hardly answer back, and there was some truth in the fact that she too had spoilt the boy. But the real reason why Diana wanted to blame Barbara was that she felt the nanny was getting too close to William, who obviously adored her. Diana was looking for an excuse to get rid of the woman who had become such an important part of William's life; too important in her view. So by the time William reached his fifth birthday, it was decided that Barbara Barnes would leave and a new nanny be employed. At first William was heart-broken when Nanny Barnes left and even his mother could not console him. But, as with every generation of Royalty, servants are considered as replaceable as furniture, so when the new woman arrived, she quickly took Nanny Barnes's place in William and Harry's affections.

Ruth Wallace had been recommended by the family of King Constantine, one of Prince Charles's closest friends (and also William's godfather), as someone who would take no nonsense from anyone, including spoilt Royal children. She

William and Harry always enjoyed the sunshine of Majorca, and in July 1998 their mother took them to stay with King Juan Carlos of Spain (seen in the left-hand photograph) at his summer home, Marivent Palace.

Opposite: *Prince Harry joins his big brother William at Wetherby School in Kensington, London, as their mother looks proudly on, September 1989.*

had worked for King Constantine's family for years and he had no hesitation in saying that she would be ideal in using a firm hand, while at the same time encouraging the children to become self-reliant. To Prince Charles's great relief, Ruth Wallace was also someone who believed in the politeness of princes. She fulfilled all Charles's hopes within weeks of her arrival.

It was also at this time that William moved schools, to Wetherby, also close to Kensington Palace where he remained for just over three years, from January 1987 until July 1990. By now his character was changing and he was popular with his contemporaries, joining in the school's activities and sports with equal enthusiasm. Having been taught to swim in the pool at Buckingham Palace when he could barely walk, it was his strongest sport and when he was seven he easily won the Grunfield Cup, awarded to the boy with the best overall style. Even at this early age, William was showing an extremely competitive side to his character. He liked winning; just taking part wasn't good enough for him. He also enjoyed still being in the limelight and had no qualms about standing on stage at school concerts and singing solo.

But it was when he moved to Ludgrove School in Berkshire in 1990 that his undoubted sporting prowess came to the fore. Taller than most of the other boys of his age, he excelled at rugby and hockey, captaining the school teams at both sports. He also enjoyed basketball and, because he had learned to shoot as a young child, soon became one of the school's stars at clay pigeon shooting. William later claimed his five years at Ludgrove were among the happiest he could remember, partly because his parents had apparently reached an amicable understanding (although they separated within two years of his joining the school) and visited their son frequently. They took part in normal parent activities such as competing in the annual father-and-son clay pigeon shoot and, a month later (this was in the summer of 1995), Diana and William took part in the mother-and-son tennis competition. They did not win but on this occasion it did not seem to matter.

It was in December 1992 that the official news of the separation of the Prince and Princess of Wales was announced in the House of Commons, but before this William's mother had visited Ludgrove, where both boys were now pupils, to break the news herself. They took it quite differently. William was devastated and broke down in tears, while Harry, who didn't fully understand the implications, was simply bewildered.

Both William and Harry could ride almost as soon as they could walk and they were introduced to hunting at a very early age. Here they join Prince Charles and Tiggy Legge-Bourke at the Beaufort Hunt in 1995.

A few months after the announcement, a young woman who was to play an important part in their lives joined the Wales's household. Alexandra Legge-Bourke, known as Tiggy, was recruited by Prince Charles to be an assistant private secretary. But, in fact, she did no administrative work and spent little time in the office. Her main task was to act as companion to Prince William and Prince Harry.

Tiggy – she is now Mrs Charles Pettifer – has an impeccable pedigree as her family has served Royalty for generations. Her mother, the Hon. Shân Legge-Bourke, is a lady-in-waiting to the Princess Royal and is also Lord Lieutenant of Powys, while her Aunt Victoria is another lady-in-waiting and was at Benenden with Princess Anne. In addition, Tiggy is a countrywoman born and bred, having been brought up on her parents' 6,000-acre estate in South Wales, where she hunts, shoots and fishes and enjoys every rural pursuit. Her mother once said, 'Tiggy could ride before she could walk.' The only thing against her as far as the Prince of Wales is concerned is that she is a chain-smoker, again just like her mother.

When Tiggy joined Prince Charles's household, William was ten years old, nervous, vulnerable and deeply suspicious of strangers. Within weeks he and Harry found they could relax totally with Tiggy and she soon became the big sister they had never had, always ready to share a joke, and her raucous laugh was often heard when she was with her young charges.

Charles could not have made a better choice. When he took the boys to Klosters skiing, Tiggy went too and as she was already an expert when they were still novices, they naturally found her to be wonderful company. Diana too welcomed Tiggy at first because she did not see her as a threat. Tiggy, on her own admission, had never been a fashion plate and was happier in jeans and sweaters than in the latest creations that Diana wore.

William and Harry used to join Tiggy and her family in Wales where they could enjoy total privacy and freedom and William came to rely on her for everything. He felt he could tell her anything and she would not laugh at him, and he could not understand when, after the first couple of years, Diana started to freeze Tiggy out. The trouble was that, when they returned to Kensington Palace, William and Harry used to talk non-stop about what they had done with Tiggy, and Diana grew jealous, feeling left out of what were obviously happy occasions. Once again William's loyalties were being tested. His mother would always occupy prime position in his affections, and that would never alter, but he also had a great liking for Tiggy and did not want to have to choose between them. He quickly learned that the best way was to keep quiet about the enjoyable evenings when he was allowed to join Prince Charles – and Tiggy – at the dinner table at Highgrove. Tiggy had never been treated like a servant, and when she was staying at Highgrove she usually joined the princes at meal times, which were highly civilized and very jolly affairs. Diana and Tiggy also had different ideas about how the boys should be brought up. Tiggy, on Prince Charles's orders, made sure they did not get everything they wanted, and that they should behave themselves as young adults, while Diana spoilt them both when they were alone with her, showering them with many of the things they should not have: chocolate, sweets, junk food and expensive presents. If William and Harry are maturing into responsible young men, much of the credit must go to Tiggy's influence in their formative years. She remained close to them through Eton, and, in William's case, university, even after leaving Prince Charles's employ, and when she married they were guests at her wedding.

Prince William, dressed all in white, attending a wedding in Herefordshire with his mother, who told him to wave at the cameras.

Where Diana and Charles differed in their views about bringing up the boys was that Diana said very early on that 'William comes first, always', whereas Charles saw the manner in which the boys were brought up was essentially to prepare them for the role they would play in their future lives. It was more important for them, especially William, to be well-mannered, cultured and taught to get on with people from all walks of life than to reach the heights academically, or even on the sports field. Prince Charles could not have cared less if either William or Harry had never played team games like football or rugby as long as they excelled at the more socially acceptable pastimes such as shooting, hunting and polo. He said he would like them brought up '. . . to think of other people, to put themselves in other people's positions . . . and even if they are not very bright, at least if they have reasonable manners they will get much further in life than by not having them'.

Princess Diana tried from the outset to equip her children to deal with conditions they might encounter beyond the confines of Royalty. She introduced them to her servants at Kensington Palace – which was not always an unqualified success, as both sides became confused at the different ways they were expected to behave when Diana was alone or when Prince Charles was present. William and Harry enjoyed going into the kitchen and having the chef show them how to make their favourite dishes. Mervyn Wycherley, who had been a chef at Buckingham Palace before moving to the Wales's household, remained with the Princess after the separation. He recalls that when the boys were quite young, they would often ask him to make them a burger, 'But it wasn't just any old burger. Theirs were always made from fillet steak, and the chips were cut from the best potatoes. There was no question of just giving

Left: *Polo is another sport the boys have always loved. Even before they were old enough to take part themselves, they would be taken to watch their father playing and in this picture William is obviously fascinated by Prince Charles's protective visor.*

Opposite: *Princess Diana holds her five-year-old son William on the steps on the Marivent Palace in Majorca during a summer holiday hosted by King Juan Carlos of Spain.*

them the sort of thing you could buy in the High Street. Though Princess Diana did like to give them a treat occasionally and take them to Burger King, which apparently they preferred to McDonalds.' In the days when Charles and Diana were together, Prince Charles did not approve of the boys' forays into the kitchen, and the young princes became apprehensive if he was around. He didn't show his disfavour to them but the staff were made aware that they should not encourage the boys to venture through the green baize door, only for them to learn the following day that Princess Diana was all for it and she would bring them in once more.

The difficulty was that Charles had never been anything other than Royal. He knew the rules and obeyed them at all times. It was automatic and he expected everyone else to adopt the same behaviour. Diana did not know the basic rules of Royalty and she was not particularly inclined to learn, and neither, in those early days, did she want her eldest son to be brought up in the stuffy atmosphere his father found so natural.

Diana was a tactile woman who loved to hug and kiss. And William was the first member of the Royal Family to be seen being cuddled in public by his mother. She saw nothing unusual in this, but the nearest Prince Charles came to showing affection in public was when he paused to pat his eldest son on the

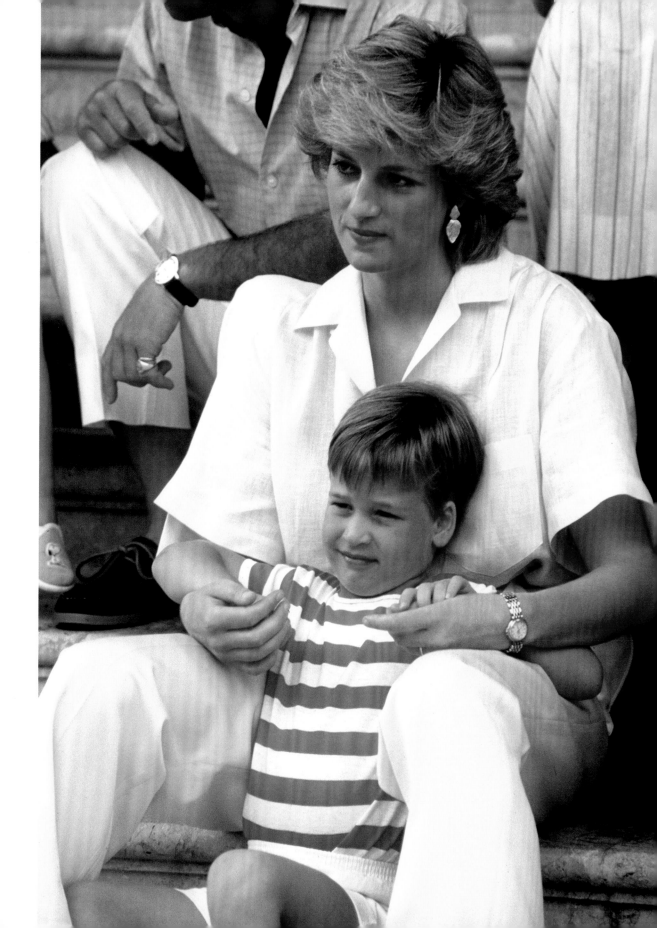

head during a polo match. It was not that Charles loved his children any less than Diana, it was simply that he was – and remains – hidebound by the conventions of Royalty that prohibits public displays of emotion. William and Harry have also been brought up with this sort of discipline, as was shown at the funerals of their mother and, five years later, Queen Elizabeth the Queen Mother. The Royal Family seems to believe it is a sign of weakness to show emotion. An old friend of The Queen told me that the only time she had ever witnessed Her Majesty close to breaking down was at the funeral service of another close, personal friend of many years standing. She said, 'I did notice The Queen blinking rather a lot.'

Another major difference in the attitudes of Diana and Charles towards their children was displayed very early on when William had to be rushed to hospital after being struck on the head by a golf club. They were both obviously very concerned, and rightly so as the boy was found to be suffering from a depressed fracture of the skull and to need an operation to relieve the pressure. Diana stayed by her son's side throughout the day and night, while Charles left for an engagement at the opera. Diana refused to leave William until she was convinced he was out of danger, remaining with him throughout

William relaxes with one of the Royal corgis after competing in the Minchinhampton Horse Trials near Princess Anne's home in May 1989.

the following day when Charles attended a conference on the environment. He saw no reason for abandoning his plans and staying with his son. It was not that he did not care. It was simply that as soon as he realized there was no further danger, he felt he should fulfil his promise to the organizers of the conference, who had made all the arrangements months before. If Charles had declined to attend at the last minute, it would have disrupted a carefully scheduled programme and would also have convinced the media that William was in a worse condition than he actually was. Nobody in the Royal Family, apart from Diana, thought there was anything strange in the decision he had taken; they would have considered it very unusual and out of character if he had altered his plans. For them, duty comes before family problems at all times. An example of this seemingly cold-hearted approach to family life occurred towards the end of 2001 when Queen Elizabeth the Queen Mother, then 101 years old and nearing the end of her long life, was taken ill and rushed into King Edward VIIth Hospital for Officers (known locally as Sister Agnes's). The Queen did not go to see her mother, remaining instead at Windsor Castle. She was kept informed of her condition but while many people thought a devoted daughter would have immediately wanted to be at her mother's side, the idea simply did not enter The Queen's head. And nobody in the Royal Family believed there was anything strange about it.

As the official biographer of the Princess Royal, I have spent many hours in her company at Gatcombe Park, her home that is a stone's throw from Highgrove. When her children were small I used to see them around the place and there was no formality at all. They could come and go as they pleased; no rooms were sacrosanct and if they made a mess it did not seem to bother the Princess one little bit. A very different situation exists in Prince Charles's home, perhaps because practically from birth he has been aware of his special position as a future sovereign and it is this that keeps him apart from even his own family.

However, since the death of Princess Diana, Charles has grown much closer to his sons. They spend lots of time together and he loves to chat with William in particular as they walk in the gardens at Highgrove. In modern parlance it is 'quality time' and is equally important to both father and son. William understands that he can learn a lot from his father and, at twenty-one, he realizes that there is still much for him to master.

SIX
Those First
Public Duties

L ike all children in the Royal Family, William was introduced to the never-ending round of public duties at an early age. But there is no such thing as formal 'on the job' training', as the Princess Royal once explained to me. 'You learn what to do and how to behave just like monkeys do, by watching your parents and doing the same as them.' And while his parents agreed that he would not undertake any Royal engagements in his own right until he has finished his education, William did accompany them on a number of their official duties from childhood, to get him used to the ceremonial aspect of Royal functions.

On the few occasions when he has appeared, William has attracted the sort of attention once reserved for his late mother. Young girls in particular treat him like a pop star and his boyish good looks, with his blue eyes tilted upwards in the same way his mother always looked, his blond hair and 6 ft 2 in height combine to make him stand out in any crowd. As he is 5 in taller than his father, with his brother fast catching up, his physical appearance comes more from the Spencer side of the family than the House of Windsor. Prince Charles is said to be delighted at the effect William has on the crowds when they go among them,

Opposite: *A little taste of early hero worship as William is given a small gift from a young admirer outside Llandaff Cathedral, Cardiff, in 1991.*

As a teenager William became used to being deluged with bunches of flowers whenever he appeared in public. He has learned to 'work the crowds' just like his mother did.

and is not in the least bit jealous as he was of Diana when she upstaged him – and the rest of the Royal Family – with no apparent effort. Looking uncannily like his late mother, with her ready smile, William is already getting used to the sort of mass hysteria and adulation that greeted her every appearance, and so far he handles his celebrity with an endearing mixture of self-assurance and good humour.

One of William's earliest public engagements occurred when he was just eight years old. Princess Diana had been invited to Cardiff to attend a service at the capital city's Llandaff Cathedral on St David's Day, 1 March 1991, and she decided to take William with her. No date or location could have been more appropriate for Prince William of Wales to be introduced to the Principality from which he takes his title.

The Royal couple were greeted on that occasion, as they were whenever either of them visited South Wales, by The Queen's representative, the Lord Lieutenant of South Glamorgan, Captain Norman Lloyd-Edwards, who subsequently enjoyed not only a dignified professional relationship with William, Harry and their mother, but a warm personal friendship that has lasted, in the case of the two princes, until today. He describes that first meeting.

I was very nervous as I had only recently been made Lord Lieutenant and it was my first major Royal visit. There were a couple of reasons why Princess Diana had been invited. The first was to mark the completion of a mammoth restoration project at Llandaff Cathedral, for which we had raised over half a

Prince William

It is never too young to learn the Royal wave, as William discovers on his first official engagement in the Principality of Wales, 1991.

million pounds, and the other was that the City of Cardiff was launching a new design for its official logo and a ceremony was planned on the same day. The problem was that the Gulf War had broken out and RAF St Athan, just a few miles from Cardiff, had been earmarked as a landing field for casualties. I was told that if this had taken place and casualties *were* at St Athan, the Princess would travel to the RAF station to comfort the wounded and meet their families. The next thing I heard from Kensington Palace was that Princess Diana wanted to bring young Prince William with her. It was to be his first public appearance in Wales – or anywhere for that matter. Of course this put the whole visit in an entirely new light. We were all thrilled to bits. And then the Prince of Wales decided he too would come as it was his son's first visit to the Principality. So this meant a change to the Order of Service, with photographs of the three Royals on the cover.

As it happened, the Gulf War ended just two days before the planned date of the visit so we were able to go ahead with our original plan – which had undergone eight drafts by now – and enjoy what turned out to be a celebration. The service in the Cathedral went like clockwork and afterwards when the Royal party signed the visitors' book it was seen for the first time that William was left-handed. No one had noticed this before that day.

It was a very full day for the eight-year-old Prince. After the church service he joined his mother (his father had left for a separate engagement) at Cardiff's

Princess Diana shows William how to sign his name in the visitors book during his first visit to Cardiff, the capital city of Wales, on St David's Day – 1 March – 1991.

St David's Hall, where they met civic dignitaries and a couple of young people dressed in carnival costumes which amused him greatly. Captain Lloyd-Edwards continues:

We stood in the wings waiting to go on stage and he was just like any other little boy. He wasn't a bit nervous. In fact he was doing most of the talking and treated me rather like an uncle he had known all his life. You'd never think we had met only a few hours before. Then after lunch, we journeyed out to RAF St Athan where Princess Diana was to meet some of the wives of those still serving in the Gulf. I thought this was going to be very boring for William so I asked the Air Commodore if there wasn't something more

William, wearing a daffodil for St David's Day, is not quite sure what to make of the two bears who join him, Princess Diana and Captain Norman Lloyd-Edwards, Lord Lieutenant of South Glamorgan, on stage as they celebrate Wales's national day, 1991.

exciting for him to see. He came up with the perfect solution – an aircraft museum. So while Princess Diana carried out her official duties, William and I toured the museum, which was God's gift to a young boy. He sat in the cockpit of a wartime Spitfire and played with all the knobs and buttons, then he did the same in a modern Harrier Jump-Jet. It was like having a private theme park to play in all by yourself. We should have stayed for just a half-hour, but I couldn't drag him away, he was enjoying himself so much. When we eventually joined up again with the official party, Diana thanked me saying, 'You're very much the flavour of the month.'

65

It was following the success of this first visit that Princess Diana decided she wanted both William and Harry to see more of Wales. After all, both their titles included 'of Wales' – Harry's full title is Prince Henry of Wales – so it was logical that they should learn something more about the country.

So later that same year Captain Lloyd-Edwards received a telephone call from the Princess telling him of her ideas and asking his help. He immediately agreed and arranged what was intended to be a private day out in Cardiff:

I was sworn to secrecy. No one was to know apart from myself and the police. I arranged to take them to three different places, including one of the world's most successful film animation studios, which I thought would fascinate them – and it did. The Princess and the boys arrived on one of the ordinary scheduled trains from London, with no special carriage, but the advance security man informed me that there were eight reporters on the train and over a dozen photographers. By the time they came off the train there were another ten press people at the station. I was very worried as I knew I hadn't told anyone. Even the people at the venues thought they were merely going to be visited by friends of mine. Of course, eventually it emerged that Diana herself had leaked the information. She knew it would be a marvellous photo-opportunity, and indeed it was.

Princess Diana had stressed that she did not want her sons to meet any official line-up of civic figures. Neither did she want a formal lunch, so Captain Lloyd-Edwards invited them to dine at his home. It turned out to be an inspired suggestion.

One of my neighbours came in to do the cooking and I found a waitress to help serve. But we didn't use the dining room, instead it was such a lovely day we ate in the conservatory. It was a simple meal, chicken and fresh vegetables, followed by apple tart and ice cream. The boys were just like two young nephews, chattering away like magpies, and before lunch Princess Diana sent them upstairs to wash their hands. I had set aside one bathroom just for her and they used the other one. Of course, this being my first occasion as host to Royalty in my own home, I was a little apprehensive, particularly with two young boys around. I thought, 'What if, like most young boys, they get bored and ask their mother, 'When are we going home' and what if they don't like the food. Children being children, they will probably say so.' But they were great, eating every morsel and even asking for second helpings of the pudding.

And when they signed the visitors' book, both boys showed a delightful sense of humour with William adding, under the heading description, 'Piggy' after his name, and Harry, 'Donkey'.

Princess Diana later became the unofficial mascot of the Welsh Rugby team and one of its most fervent supporters. She insisted on bringing William and Harry to international matches at Cardiff's Millennium Stadium, when they joined in the community singing, even learning the Welsh national anthem in Welsh. After her death, the boys continued to visit South Wales, but not as frequently as before. Prince Charles brought them to one rugby match, but it was not the same as when Diana was alive. However, on one occasion, at an

In fine voice at the National Stadium in Cardiff before an international rugby match. Diana, William and Harry all signed the picture and dedicated it to Norman Lloyd-Edwards as 'The best singer in the Front Row.'

Left: *William was just six years old when he first attended the Trooping the Colour ceremony in London. Here he is seen riding in an open carriage to Horseguards to watch his grandmother The Queen take the salute.*

Below: *William and Harry, with three of their cousins, being given a special treat – a ride around the inner quadrangle at Buckingham Palace in one of The Queen's carriages.*

official lunch before an important game with New Zealand, William and Harry had been presented with various badges by the Welsh Rugby Union, which they proudly wore on their lapels. Norman Lloyd-Edwards was present when one of the top officials from the visiting side offered a New Zealand badge: 'They were having none of it. William accepted his graciously, but Harry – who was much younger of course – refused saying "I am Welsh today, I don't want anyone else's badge." Thankfully, the President of the New Zealand Rugby Union took it in good part and didn't take offence so a potential "international incident" was averted. William told Harry he should accept it, after all New Zealand was in the Commonwealth, but he was adamant.'

William and Harry were brought to Cardiff during the millennium celebrations and Harry was given the opportunity of talking to one of his sporting heroes face to face. Again it was Norman Lloyd-Edwards who arranged the meeting: 'I knew he would be bored stiff just meeting all the officials when it was the players he was really interested in, so I took him to meet the Captain of the Welsh team, Robert Howley. At that time, Harry was playing rugby at Eton and to listen to these two talking about the finer points of the game was a brilliant experience for an outsider. They got on so well and later he told me he had enjoyed the chat better than almost anything he could remember.'

An occasion when Norman Lloyd-Edwards witnessed William enjoying a warm friendship with one of the newest members of the Royal Family also occurred during a rugby match in Cardiff: 'Wales were playing Scotland in February 1996 and William and Harry came with the Prince of Wales and Tim Laurence. One thing that impressed me on that Saturday afternoon was the way in which Tim and William got on. They obviously liked each other very much and Prince William spent most of the afternoon chatting with Tim. There was an easy relationship between them that was very pleasant to see and if Tim seemed cautious with the rest of the party, he certainly was fully at ease with the young Prince.'

Looking back over the years Captain Lloyd-Edwards has known William, and seen him mature from an eight-year-old child to a young adult, he has had a unique insight into the character of the man who one day will be King:

He wasn't like any other boy. Even as a youngster there was a calmness about him that made him stand apart from everyone else. It wasn't something he had to work at, it was bred into him, a natural dignity that is,

The Prince of Wales and Prince William sign a book of condolence in Edinburgh for those killed in the terrorist attack on the World Trade Centre in New York on 11 September 2001.

to say the least, unusual in a teenager, and on top, he has always shown an enormous sense of responsibility. Added to which, he has shouldered the responsibility of looking after Harry, as a younger brother, since the death of their mother. They were absolutely devoted to Princess Diana and were devastated when she died. I think that since then William has become even more of a figure for Harry to look up to than is usual with two brothers. They are much closer than the average brothers of their age and while Harry is the more outgoing of the pair, William has had to learn to cope with the media and the public. It hasn't come easily. He hates having his photograph taken and I remember on one occasion being in the car with Princess Diana and William when he put his hands in front of his face to avoid the cameras.

Opposite: *Prince Charles gives his son William an affectionate kiss during the celebrations in Hyde Park to mark the fiftieth anniversary of VE Day (Victory in Europe Day) in 1995.*

His mother said, 'Take your hands away Wills, you'll have to get used to this. It's never going to go away.'

Norman Lloyd-Edwards was present at one of the most frantic scenes of 'Willsmania' when Prince Charles and his elder son carried out an impromptu walk-about after a religious service at a Welsh chapel: 'It was like something out of the Beatles. Girls were screaming "William, William, come over here", all the time. It was deafening. They threw bunches of flowers at him and climbed over each other trying to touch him. He handled it brilliantly, and secretly, I felt he didn't mind it at all. As a baptism of fire, it could not have been more successful and Prince Charles was delighted that William "worked the crowd" as well as his mother used to.'

Members of the Royal Family are often asked to become godparents. Prince Charles has lost count of the number of godchildren he has, but every one receives a card and present on his or her birthday, and he is kept informed of their progress at school and their spiritual development. This responsibility has also been passed on to William, who was just sixteen when he became a godfather for the first time. One of Prince William's godfathers, King Constantine of the Hellenes, now resides in London where William is a frequent and welcome guest at his home in Hampstead. So in 1998, he was delighted to accept the invitation to become godfather to King Constantine's grandson, Konstantine Alexios, the second child of Crown Prince and Crown Princess Pavlos. William is the youngest of the eight godparents and the closest in age to his godson. Prince Charles is godfather to the baby's sister, Maria-Olympia. The Crown Prince and Princess were anxious to have a representative of the British Royal Family as a godparent to each child as the Crown Prince grew up in Britain. Konstantine was christened on 15 April at the Greek Cathedral in London with representatives of the Royal houses of Greece, Denmark, Sweden and Yugoslavia present. King Constantine gave a celebration dinner afterwards at Claridges at which William, whose left arm was in a sling following a sporting injury, was forced to eat with only his right hand.

It is fairly obvious that William already has the Windsors' sense of duty, but he also possesses the charisma and indefinable 'star quality' of the late Princess of Wales. Together they will prove a formidable combination in the years to come.

seven
Eton

L ong before he was born, decisions were taken regarding William's upbringing, education, introduction into public life and career until he eventually becomes King. He has little control over his future and virtually no say in the route it will take. He *was* asked if he would like to go to Eton, but as Princess Anne said when the time came for her to go away to Benenden School, 'I liked the idea of going away to school with other girls, but it wouldn't have made the slightest difference to the outcome if I had objected.' Similarly, when the choice of schools for William was being discussed, there was no chance of the decision being altered if he had said he did not want to go to Eton.

As it happened, it was a happy choice, even if Prince Philip never quite got over his disappointment that William did not go to Gordonstoun, the Scottish public school he and all three of his sons had attended with different degrees of affection and success. It has been well documented that Prince Charles hated his time at Gordonstoun with its spartan regime of cold baths and early morning cross-country runs. So he was delighted to fall in with the suggestions of his wife and grandmother that his own son should go to the most famous school in the world.

Eton is where the children of the nation's elite have been educated for centuries and the college also happens to be conveniently placed for Windsor Castle, where William often joined The Queen for Sunday afternoon tea. When William started at the school the fees were £5,220 a term.

William's first day at Eton, 1995. He was delighted to be going there as many of his friends from his preparatory school were also pupils at the most famous college in the world.

Opposite: *William was accompanied by his parents and his brother when he arrived at Eton for the first time in September 1995 to meet the man who would be his housemaster, Dr Andrew Gailey.*

The Queen Mother used her influence to persuade Charles and Diana when they were trying to decide which school William should attend after nursery and prep. She never doubted for a moment that Eton was the right – indeed the only – place for her great-grandson. Prince Charles did not want William to go to Gordonstoun, so he readily fell in with the suggestion, and Diana – whose family connections with the school stretched back generations – had always said it was where she wanted her sons to go. Besides, she wanted them near to her, and Scotland was too far away. The Queen would have liked the boys to follow in their paternal grandfather's steps, if only to please Prince Philip, but she knew when she was beaten, and privately was delighted at the prospect of having William near Windsor Castle. In this way, she knew she could keep a friendly eye on him and continue his ongoing training for his eventual role as

King. The Queen Mother thought she had made the choice alone, but in reality, whoever made the decision, it worked out well for almost all concerned.

Chris Patten, a former Minister of Education and an old friend of the Prince of Wales, was not involved in the initial decision to send William to Eton, but he is in no doubt that it was the best option:

I think Eton is good for everyone. It's an outstanding school. It produces young men who have self-confidence without being bumptious. And it instils a charm that is an admirable mix of wit, scholarship, *noblesse oblige* and urbanity that it appears to be fashionable to criticize or lampoon today. It was a very sensible decision to send him there. The boys who go there are an amazing mix of types and cultures, races and religions. I remember going to speak there and finding out that they had a German master who taught Mandarin. One of his pupils was the grandson of the former head of China's security service. Where else could you get such an eclectic bunch? Eton is a school that offers something for everyone: tradition, discipline and discretion.

William was quite pleased. He knew a lot of boys who were either already at the school or were joining at the same time as him, so he was not going to be thrown alone in at the deep end. He also told his great-grandmother she had made the right choice. Even at that age he knew how to say to people what they wanted to hear. When he learned he was going to spend five years at Eton he is said to have made one request: that he should be allocated a room 'with a view of the Castle so I can see Grannie'.

William enjoyed his schooldays, excelling at sports, becoming co-captain of Eton's swimming team in his final year. The other boys did not have to bow to him or call him Prince William. To them he was just William Wales; his swimming costume and tracksuit bore the legend 'W.O.W.' for William of Wales. He didn't have many privileges not shared by his contemporaries, but there

The left-handed Prince William signs the schoolbook watched over by his parents and Prince Harry on his first day at Eton College.

William wore the distinctive regulation Eton uniform of black tail coat, striped trousers, waistcoat and white bow tie, which dates back to the death of King George III in 1820 when the College went into mourning for His Majesty.

was one important luxury his fellow pupils at Manor House would have appreciated. He was the only boy at Eton to have a private bathroom. Otherwise he followed exactly the same regime as everyone else, and asked for nothing more.

The Prince's room was a typical English public-school, cell-like study-cum-bedroom measuring just 4 m by 3 m. As decoration William broke the rules by having tie-dye drapes pinned to the walls; these were banned on the grounds that they were a fire hazard. There was a narrow single bed with above it a signed poster of his favourite band of the time, All Saints, and, as he grew a little older, thirteen pin-ups, including supermodel Cindy Crawford and tennis star Anna Kournikova in an array of revealing underwear. The walls were plastered with the posters of a typical teenager. One bright yellow one carried the warning 'Don't Drink and Drive – Smoke a Spliff and Fly', while another boasted 'Instant Idiot – just add alcohol'.

An empty bottle of Grand Vin de Château Latour, vintage 1966 – the year England won the World Cup – was displayed on his dressing table and there was another picture of his favourite soccer team, Aston Villa, pinned to the wall. Intriguingly, an illegible signature was scrawled on another poster from a skiing holiday with the note 'William: This is to remember Spring. Exhilaration next time.' It has never been explained what this note meant or whom it was from. William was a member of Eton's Army cadet force and his Army equipment was kept in a distinctly utility wardrobe with his purple and green services sleeping mat rolled up in another corner of the room.

The Prince's bureau-type desk contained his school work with pride of place going to two photographs: the first of his mother wearing a red jacket and the other a full-length portrait in a solid silver frame of Prince Charles in a Guards uniform. These pictures were to accompany William wherever he went. In every room he occupies, there are invariably photographs of his parents. At Eton William wore the regulation uniform of black tailcoat, waistcoat, striped

William, Diana and Harry enjoying the cold fresh air of Lech as they ride in a horse-drawn sleigh in March 1993.

Princess Diana loved to ski and she instilled the same passion in her children. Here she is with William in the fashionable Austrian resort of Lech just before they take to the slopes in 1993. At this time he was a boarder at Ludgrove Preparatory School.

trousers and white bow tie, which dates back to the death of King George III in 1820 when the college went into mourning for His Majesty.

Eton is unique among Britain's public schools in that the curriculum includes not only the normal academic subjects and classic languages such as Greek and Latin, but also offers tuition in Chinese Mandarin, Japanese and Arabic and such disparate subjects as car maintenance and cookery. There are 1,260 pupils enrolled in the 24 houses of approximately fifty boys, and each and every pupil is allocated an individual tutor. William's was Christopher Stuart-Clarke, whose main subject was English but who was required to supervise William's entire academic programme. This took the form of a weekly two-hour informal discussion during which the young man's progress, which had previously been reported by his class tutors, was examined and William also had an opportunity to raise any problems he might have encountered during the previous seven days. Initially he also received a lot of support from the matron of Manor House, Elizabeth Heathcote, known as 'the Dame'.

When William first arrived at the school, his parents had already separated and he was a very uncertain and unhappy thirteen-year-old. Within a year Charles and Diana were divorced, adding to William's unsettled outlook, but his fellow pupils handled the news with assurance and nonchalance. They couldn't have cared less who his parents were or what they got up to. Royalty had been present at Eton for generations, and when William became the child of divorced parents he actually became one of a large minority. There was nothing new or unusual in having parents who had split up.

William was fortunate in his housemaster Dr Andrew Gailey. He knew exactly how to handle the young Prince, protecting him without appearing to do so and at the same time making sure he did not receive any privileges denied the other boys in Manor House. What was quite remarkable was that although William enjoyed his five years at Eton, they were years when the Royal Family, and his parents in particular, were going through the worst period in their lives. Divorces, scandals and revelations about the private life of the royals brought the reputation of the monarchy to its lowest point – until the death of Diana in 1997 caused it to plummet to the very depths. Yet in spite of the news stories that appeared almost on a daily basis revealing another juicy scandal, William remained untouched. The school was the perfect place for a young man to mix with other boys whose parents came from a wide variety of backgrounds; even if most were comfortably well off. There were some who came from more modest families, as Eton has a system whereby approximately 200 boys are selected from state schools when they are ten years old and the College pays for them to go to preparatory school before they go up to Eton itself, where they continue to receive assistance with their fees. In this way they are integrated into the College in a way that is less of a culture shock than it might be if they went directly from their state school. So it meant that William was mixing with boys from comparatively humble homes as well as with the sons of the rich and famous. It was his first experience of communal living and he found it quite to his liking. He also very quickly developed the self-assured manner of his peers. What he particularly liked about Eton was the fact that he could be the same as his fellow pupils, with one fundamental difference of course. He was the only one, until Harry joined him, whose grandmother was Queen.

Prince William did have to put up with having his personal police bodyguard around at all times. Fortunately the man appointed to guard him was married with two sons of his own, so he knew how to handle boys. Sergeant Graham Cracker lived in a room adjoining William's at Eton but he understood how important it was to allow the young Prince as much freedom as possible. Cracker was the sole of discretion and when William strolled over the bridge into Windsor town with his pals, he kept to a discreet distance. All the other boys at Eton knew who he was, of course, and they did their best to ignore him, which is what he wanted. The difficulty in a place like Eton is that the village and the adjoining town of Windsor are magnets for tourists; there was no way of shutting areas off from visitors or residents, as main roads open to the public at all times run through school and town, so protecting the future heir to the throne was not always the easiest of tasks.

Until William was seventeen, Sergeant Cracker always drove him wherever he wanted to go. Once he obtained a provisional driving licence, he hated being driven by anyone. Generally speaking the Prince and his minder got on very well. There were the occasional disagreements, usually because William wanted to go to a party and be left alone, or because he had met a pretty girl and felt the presence of the policeman was ruining his chances. But Graham Cracker knew his job and he also realized that it would not be to anyone's benefit for him to try and forge a closer relationship. As far as he was concerned, he was an employee of the Metropolitan Police Force who was there solely to protect his

young charge. He was not an uncle figure or older brother and William was by now mature enough to recognize that his bodyguard was not someone he could lean on. In 2002, he was to learn to his cost that if a member of the Royal Family allowed anyone to get too close, as his late mother had done with Ken Wharfe, who wrote a scandalous book about his time as bodyguard to Diana and her sons, the danger was always there. Wharfe is the only former police officer to reveal intimate secrets of his years guarding Royalty and he waited to do so until a few weeks after he had retired, much to the disgust of many of his former colleagues.

In Dr Gailey's house William learned how to streamline his culinary skills, but his housemates all said only they knew how many sausages and strips of bacon he burnt before he could honestly claim to cook a decent 'full English' breakfast. He liked cooking, which was just as well for after he had left Eton and was in Belize on his gap year in the jungle, he was forced to take his turn preparing meals for the team.

Perhaps the main reason for his success at Eton was his undoubted prowess at sports. By the time he was a sixth former, he was already 6 ft 2 in tall, a great help on the football field and in the swimming pool. He captained Gailey's team in inter-house soccer matches and played rugby for the schools 2nd XV until a hand injury in 1998 stopped him playing for good. Perhaps he had been told of his Uncle Edward's (the Earl of Wessex) problems when he was at Cambridge. Edward was a more than useful forward until he discovered there was an undercover society called the Get Edward Group whose sole aim was to inflict serious injury on him during matches. He soon realized there was little point in continuing to play after being bitten several times and he gave the game up.

It was in the swimming pool that William really excelled. As a junior he won the 50 m and 100 m titles and as a senior he captained the school swimming team. At Eton they call the captain the Keeper of Swimming. William swam every day during term and most other days in the pool at Buckingham Palace, where they have an unwritten rule regarding the use of the pool. The Queen allows members of the household to use the pool if no member of the Royal Family wants it. If a household member is already in when one of the family

Opposite: *A thoughtful pose as William is pictured relaxing in the prefects' common room at Eton in June 2000.*

Eton

Prince William chats with his godfather, King Constantine, at the christening of His Majesty's grandson Konstantine Alexios, in 1998.

In 1998, while still at Eton, William was delighted to be asked to become godfather to King Constantine's grandson, Konstantine Alexios, the second child of Crown Prince and Crown Princess Pavlos, although his left arm was in a sling as a result of a sporting injury. The christening took place on 15 April at the Greek Cathedral in London.

turns up, they always get out immediately, unless invited to remain. If the family member is swimming when one of the household arrives, he or she does not enter the water. Princess Diana was the most frequent swimmer in the days when she was still a close family member and she would often invite anyone swimming when she turned up to remain and join her. William prefers to swim alone, but if the member of the household is someone he knows and likes he will sometimes allow them to stay. Diana was an accomplished swimmer herself and no doubt would have been delighted and proud of her elder son's aquatic achievements.

At Eton William loved the rough and tumble of water polo, playing at least twice a week in his position of 'Up Front' where he could be sure to see plenty of the action. No shrinking violet, either in the pool or on the playing fields, he enjoyed the admiration of his schoolmates. They, in turn, respected his prowess and the fact that he neither asked for nor gave any quarter. Not that it would have mattered if he had. Etonians – and most other public schoolboys – are notoriously unaffected by rank. Children as a rule do not suffer the same self-seeking ambition as many of their parents. That comes later in life.

The Prince's group of personal friends included his cousin, Lord Frederick Windsor (Freddie), the son of Prince and Princess Michael of Kent. He became something of an extra 'unofficial' bodyguard, warding off unwanted attention from intrusive onlookers who tried to get too close when the boys attended Sunday afternoon polo matches at Smith's Lawn, Windsor. And there were also several other boys of his own age who had been at Ludgrove with him.

One of the skills William learned while at Eton was how to use a computer. He did not have his own laptop, but his house boasted four computers and he spent hours surfing the net and working on systems that he may never use but which have given him considerable satisfaction.

Although Eton accepts boys of every faith, it is unashamedly Christian in its teaching, outlook and, indeed, foundation. The prospectus informs all parents of would-be pupils that 'Eton College was founded . . . for the worship of God and for the training of young men to the service of the Church and State', in that order. This was the main reason why the late Queen Mother was so insistent on her great-grandson attending the College and why The Queen and Prince Charles readily agreed. It is the perfect establishment for a future King to learn the basic facts of the Church of which he will one day be the Supreme Governor.

Eton

If William has any doubts about the spiritual aspects of his future role, he has only to look at the example of the founder of Eton, his ancestor Henry VI, whose whole life was devoted to service and prayer.

While religious instruction plays an important part in the daily life of the College – all boys are required to attend Chapel unless they are practising members of another faith when alternative arrangements are made – there is nothing dull or typically 'Church of England' about the way it is taught. Far from the days of fifty or sixty years ago when morning prayers at school were boring affairs mostly learned parrot-fashion, and just as quickly forgotten, at Eton there is a light-hearted approach to the subject. As well as the orthodox teaching there are talks and debates on subjects such as sex, contraception and relationships. The boys are encouraged to join in – and they do with enthusiasm – and nothing seems to be taboo. On one occasion, there was even a discussion about what sort of woman a future sovereign should take as a partner in life. William received all sorts of advice, all accepted in good part, although he declined to comment, knowing that if he did, it might somehow appear later in a newspaper.

During his five years at Eton, William served in the school's Officer Training Corps (OTC), but he showed no great enthusiasm for the drills and manoeuvres. It was really a matter of following the tradition whereby all royal males undertake some form of military training. Nevertheless, it will stand him in good stead if he eventually enters one of the armed forces for a time.

One achievement that gave William great satisfaction was being elected to Pop, an elite group of sixth formers who rule the roost at Eton. His fellow prefects chose him to join their number and without their voluntary consent and approval he could not have reached the heights to which all Etonians aspire. One of the privileges enjoyed by members of Pop is to wear a waistcoat of their own design – the more outlandish the better. William had several made for him by his Savile Row tailor, Tom Gilbey, including one patriotic waistcoat displaying the Union Jack.

Prince Charles told William many times that although he should enjoy his school days, there was still work to be done. It was important that his examination grades should match those of his colleagues so that no one could later accuse him of being shown favouritism when he applied to go to university. By his own admission William is not particularly gifted academically, but he

As a sixth former and a prefect William could wear a non-regulation waistcoat to show his individuality. He had several made by his Savile Row tailor.

worked hard at his lessons taking three A levels, gaining an A in geography, a B in history and a C in biology. This would not have been enough to earn him a place at Oxbridge, but that was not on the agenda anyway.

In the meantime, William had decided, with his father's agreement, that he would take a year off before going up to university, and plans for his gap year involved meetings, discussions and endless preparations regarding what to do, where to go and with whom.

Eton

eight
Gap
Year

William's gap year was divided into segments and, as with every other aspect of his life, a number of people were involved in deciding where he should go and in what role. Chris Patten was one of those consulted by the Prince of Wales and took the view that a gap year should comprise three elements: 'The first was travel, and to the most exotic places we could think of. I think, and everyone seemed to agree, that this would make the whole project more exciting. Then there had to be an element of adventure, even danger perhaps. And thirdly, to get the most out of the year, some form of educational aspect had to be included.'

William's father particularly wanted him to gain some experience of service life, so the first part of the gap year was spent on exercise with the Welsh Guards in the jungles of Belize. The British Army and Royal Marines use the area for specialist jungle training – Prince Edward described the week he spent there with 40 Commando in 1985 one of the most 'hellish weeks of my life'. William was to find it equally unwelcoming.

The jungle is steamy, humid, hot, permanently wet and in most places impenetrable. In other words, perfect for its purpose. Before he travelled to Belize, William had to be inoculated against the various tropical diseases prevalent in the area and he was given a crash course in emergency treatment for snakebite. He was warned by his companion, Winston Harris, an experienced Belizean jungle fighter, what to do if he was bitten by a poisonous snake. He was told to cut off its head with a machete and keep the body so that doctors could measure it and thereby assess how much venom had been passed into his body. Not the most encouraging start to his stay.

William did not ask for, nor would he have been given, any special treatment. His quarters were exactly the same as the others on the course – which was codenamed Native Trail. His bed was a hammock slung between two trees, with particular attention paid to the presence of any possible intruders such as snakes and poisonous insects. This was not an attempt at scaremongering by his instructors. As they pointed out, every year up to fifty men were airlifted back to Britain suffering from some form of attack from animals, reptiles or the disease-ridden environment.

One thing William was quite relieved he did not have to do himself was kill a pig. But the non-commissioned officers running the exercise showed his squad how it was done, and how to butcher the carcass afterwards. He did, however, have to use his machete to kill and gut a chicken and cook it over an open fire, though he drew the line at eating it raw, as soldiers sometimes have to do when they are in action. Another 'appetising' titbit was termite stew, which he did manage to eat – and keep down.

William was already an excellent shot before he went to Belize but he had never handled semi-automatic weapons before, and he was glad of the opportunity to get to grips with a variety of guns. One of his instructors, Corporal Claud Martinez of the Belize Defence Force, said, 'The Prince would make a good soldier. . . . He was surrounded by men firing machine-guns and still he looked at ease. I never saw a moment of panic on his face.'

On his return to Britain William held his first ever press conference at Highgrove. His father was at his side, but William had obviously gained a great deal of confidence from his experience in Belize. He played down the dangers he had faced and merely said, when asked to talk about his time there, 'I was with the Welsh Guards on exercise in the jungle, training with them and seeing what they do.' William also explained how he had received the news of his A level examination results while he was in Belize. 'I was in the middle of nowhere. The base camp where I was staying was up the hill – I got a message – the only way to get the A level results was to have them delivered over the Army net. The guys did not want to use it, so I got a message that Dr Gailey, my housemaster, was waiting with what he said was good news, so I raced back up the hill.' In fact

From the village where he stayed in Chile as part of his gap year, William had a magnificent view of the Andes. He said it was breathtaking and something he wouldn't have missed for anything.

Opposite: *William shared exactly the same accommodation as his team mates in Chile. There was no concession to his Royal status – and he wouldn't have accepted it if it had been offered.*

it was Prince Charles who had sent an e-mail, the first time he had successfully used the system, and he was delighted, both with the results and with the fact that he had mastered what had been up until then an electronic mystery.

The next stage of this carefully arranged gap year was to see William in an entirely different and much more pleasant environment. The Royal Geographical Society was running a programme called Shoals of Capricorn, which was intended to teach marine conservation. William travelled to the island of Rodrigues, some 300 miles south-east of Mauritius in the Indian Ocean. When he arrived on the island, he could not have found a greater contrast with the jungles of Belize. Here there were empty white beaches, palm trees and soft cool breezes in one of the world's most peaceful locations. And, in a moment of wry humour, William decided to register on the island as plain Brian Woods for his month-long stay. The authorities obviously had to be told who he was but most of the islanders were completely unaware of their new guest's identity.

William stayed in a small lodge where the rate was £25 a night, including breakfast. A half-hour drive from Port Mathurin, the main town of the island, Le Domaine de Decide, was the ideal base. Here he could be left alone but it was not too far if he wanted to ride his hired 125cc Honda moped, which he used daily to get around the island's primitive roads. Waiting for him back home was a much more powerful motor bike, a present from his father as a reward for his good A level results.

One of the ways in which the locals fished the waters around Rodrigues was to use dynamite to blow the fish to the surface and then simply haul in the catch. They did not realize how damaging to the environment this method was, and William tried, without too much success, to show them the error of their ways. He also scuba-dived to see how much damage was being done to the coral reef and in one of his off-duty moments tried to teach some of the native lads how to play rugby. He later recalled how difficult it was when '. . . neither of you speaks the other's language.' During one of these lessons a photographer took some pictures of him and it was really only then that the people of Rodrigues began to realize who was among them.

The Prince's month in the Indian Ocean was perhaps the most enjoyable and relaxing part of his gap year. The next instalment was certainly not in that category.

William and a team mate building wooden walkways linking buildings in Tortel.

Opposite: *Paintbrush in hand, William varnishes the outside of the local radio station in Tortel.*

Prince Charles was a supporter of Raleigh International and had been one of the moving forces behind its original expedition in 1984 along with the explorer Colonel John Blashford Snell. Charles felt that one of their overseas expeditions would be an ideal way for William to gain experience with other young people of his own age – and more importantly – from different backgrounds and nationalities. At Eton he had been allowed to develop his own personality and gather a circle of friends around him. But they came mostly from the aristocracy, or at least from among the wealthiest families. This would be entirely new. He was offered a choice of locations for a ten-week stint that would, according to the Raleigh brochure, 'Inspire people from all backgrounds and nationalities to discover their full potential by working together on

Tortel resident ten-year-old Marcella Hernadez-Rioz photographed during an English lesson with her Royal tutor, who jokes with her as they practise.

Prince William

William thoroughly enjoyed meeting the village youngsters at Tortel Nursery and during a lunch break he gave a shoulder ride to six-year-old Alejandro Heredia who was determined the future King would not see where they were going.

challenging environmental and community projects around the world.' This was exactly what Prince Charles had hoped for his elder son and he was confident that the experience would broaden his outlook and hold him in good stead during his ongoing training for future kingship.

Before he was able to join the expedition, William had to attract sponsorship to pay for the trip. He organized a water polo match, which raised £5,500, and Prince Charles matched the figure as a contribution to Raleigh's programme for disadvantaged young people. Of all the countries he was offered, among them Mongolia, Namibia and Ghana, William selected Chile. The decision was his and fortunately the Palace approved. It was a part of the world he was curious about and that he had never visited or even heard much about, and he was convinced that by opting to work in a remote village location, no one would know who he was. That was very important to him. He wanted to get away from all the attention he had been receiving and he insisted that no entourage should accompany him. His personal police protection officer had to be with him at all times, and in permanent contact with the Palace through his satellite telephone. But William was without a valet or any other servant to do his fetching and carrying. It would prove to be a salutary but ultimately rewarding experience.

When he was teaching English to the children of Tortel, William wrote on a whiteboard using the affectionate nickname 'Wombat', which his mother used to call him.

William had to turn his hand to whatever needed doing. He is seen here making a rubbish bin for the villagers.

He said, 'I chose Chile because I wanted to go somewhere colder rather than hotter.' He could not have chosen better. It was cold, wet and during the first week they never once saw the sun.

The first part of the expedition was easily the worst. The twelve young men and women in the group found the atrocious weather conditions and the inhospitable terrain in the southern hills of Patagonia tested their stamina and patience to the limit. When he returned to Britain William revealed what the first week had been like: 'On the first day, we paddled in our kayaks against a rising storm for three hours simply to reach the first scheduled land base, a safe beach where we could pull up our kayaks away from the seas. We had

Opposite: The first week of William's stay in Chile was wet, cold and miserable. But by the time this picture was taken things had improved considerably and he was able to see the funny side of the expedition.

hardly finished that task when the rain began to come down in torrents.' And it was unlike rain any of them had experienced before:

> . . . the rain never stopped for five days and five nights. You go to bed, you wake up, it's still raining. We were all soaked through. . . . We had to go to bed each night in wet clothes but, thank goodness, my sleeping bag remained dry, which was a great relief. Eventually, even the tent became wet through; it was saturated. In the end we became quite demoralised even though we somehow managed to keep ourselves going by singing, telling jokes and stories. . . . Of course we also had to eat and try to keep warm. Some of the venturers so hated the rain they stayed in their tents all day and all night. . . . That meant that a few of us had to take it in turns to go out into the blinding rain, chopping and collecting firewood. . . . The thing was, I'd never seen rain like that before in my life. It was so heavy and just didn't stop. To make matters worse, there was a howling wind as well – the tents were flapping around and almost blowing away. It was touch and go . . . it became quite demoralising. I think we all felt wretched. Everyone was thinking to themselves, 'Why? Why did I choose to come here?' But somehow we managed to get through it and that was good.

This was intended to be the adventure section of the stay in Chile and, as William later put it, 'It was bloody awful, ghastly.' There was nothing enjoyable about those first few days. Everything was wet through, the food was appalling, they had to make their own fires – when they could collect enough dry firewood to burn – and everybody's spirits were low. It would have been perfectly understandable if some, perhaps all of them, had decided to call it a day and give up. But none of them did and the thought simply did not cross William's mind. One of his colleagues on the expedition said, 'Whatever you say about him, he is not a quitter.' Luckily after the first week the rain subsided and they were able to dry their clothes and tents and start to enjoy themselves. As William remarked, '. . . we had almost forgotten what a hot meal tasted like. Food has never tasted as good as that first decent meal after the rain had stopped.'

As an introduction to the harsher side of life beyond the confines of palace, castle and even public school, it could not have been more effective. William later said it was a great experience but one he would not rush to repeat.

nine
At
Home

Prince William has always considered it important to have his own space. When he lived with his mother at Kensington Palace, he shared the nursery with Harry but there were days when he wanted to be on his own, and both his nanny and Diana realized that the need for privacy was a vital part of his make-up and respected this even when he was too young to protest if they had not agreed.

At Eton, William's study was sacrosanct; nobody was allowed in unless invited. Doors were usually left open, but if his was closed it meant, stay out. When he started at St Andrews University, his rooms in the hall of residence were fitted out comfortably but not luxuriously. Again they were the Prince's private domain where he liked to retreat at the end of the day and play records, watch television and read. Then in September 2002, William decided to leave and set up home in the town of St Andrews with three friends. They rented a flat in one of the most desirable areas. It was already furnished, but William brought his own bed and several items he had salvaged from the Royal storerooms at Windsor.

William also has his own suite of rooms at York House, St James's Palace, his father's 75-room apartment (soon to be vacated when he takes up residence across the road in Clarence House). William is on the top floor and this is where he brings friends at weekends or after a late party in London. When he was first given the suite – while still at Eton – there was a

A rare official, if informal, photocall for William, who dislikes being photographed. This picture was taken at Highgrove when he and Prince Charles spoke about his gap year activities.

disagreement with Prince Charles when he brought a group of school friends home late one night and invited them to 'crash out' on the floor in their sleeping bags. Prince Charles was angry; not because the friends were there, but because William hadn't bothered to let the staff know in advance that he and some friends were coming. They had to provide meals at the last minute and Prince Charles thought it extremely bad manners for his son to place his staff in this position. William never did it again.

The Prince's bedroom at Highgrove is a calm oasis overlooking the garden and curiously formal for a young student on the brink of adulthood. Unlike those of some of his contemporaries, William's room does not boast black walls, purple carpets or psychedelic images but is sand-coloured with complementary pastel shades throughout. It has its own adjoining bathroom. He likes to perch on the window seat, his favourite spot. He says this is where he does most of his thinking, surrounded by family photographs: The Queen and Prince Philip, Prince Charles and Diana (in happier times). There is one of himself and Harry taken at Balmoral and another sent by one of his favourite cousins, Lady Sarah Chatto, Princess Margaret's daughter.

In keeping with the Scottish theme that runs throughout every Royal residence, there is a watercolour of a scene in the Highlands and a portrait of Prince Rupert, a Royalist cavalry commander, mounted on his charger during the Civil War. In Royal homes pictures of Oliver Cromwell or his forces are not greatly in evidence. The bathroom contains one of William's special favourites: a poster of the American supermodel Christie Brinkley.

Although he is very much his mother's son in physical appearance, William shares his father's Royal attitudes to domestic matters. Diana would often pop into the kitchen at Kensington Palace or Highgrove – when she still lived there – and chat informally with the servants. Charles would never dream of doing that and neither these days would William. When he and Harry were small and living with their mother they also liked to go unannounced into the kitchen and see what was going on. And the staff liked them to do so. As William put it, 'Life with Mummy was totally informal. We could do as we liked; run into the kitchen and ask the cook for a Coke or a burger [made with fillet steak of course] at any time.' But since Diana's death, with the boys now living with their father, all traces of such casualness have disappeared. William prefers to keep the servants at arm's length. There is no arrogance in his manner, but everyone is aware of his status and the staff also prefer it this way. They know exactly where they are with him, unlike when Diana was alive and there would be familiarity one day and frigid formality the next. The idea of William and Harry having pillow fights with anyone, as they used to with Diana and later with Tiggy, would be unthinkable today. There is a new sense of discipline about the household since Camilla Parker Bowles brought her influence to bear.

In a written interview with the Press Association William revealed several details about his private life. He said his favourite pet was his black Labrador, Widgeon, and he enjoys drawing, painting, silver-working and playing video games. An unusual pastime for a prince with such a sporting reputation is that he likes reading poetry. He also enjoys pop music and action movies. William's favourite memento of his mother is said to be her Cartier wrist watch.

William is a true Royal in that he loves the country, without wishing to completely abandon the delights of city life. He enjoys walking in the garden at Highgrove, but on his own admission is no gardener, unlike his father and great-grandmother, who believed that only if you get your hands dirty could you call yourself a true lover of the country. The Queen regards herself as a real countrywoman, but no one can ever recall seeing her on her hands and knees planting or weeding, so possibly William gets his feelings about such activities from her. An annual visit to the Chelsea Flower Show is a Royal duty and one

A reminder of happier times. Prince Charles with William and Harry on holiday in Scotland in the summer of 1997 just before they learned of the death of Diana, Princess of Wales.

Right: *William in Scotland in September 2001 as he is about to start a four-year course in History of Art at St Andrews University.*

Below: *The heir to the throne sitting between his two sons as they are carried up the slopes in a chair-lift before skiing down again, Canada, 1997.*

At Home

The Queen enjoys, and William, who has not yet had to include this occasion in his diary, may well feel the same when the time comes.

William has grown to love Highgrove. He feels it is a real home at last. When he was younger and his parents were constantly rowing, he dreaded weekends, not knowing if he was going to be at Highgrove with his father or at Kensington Palace with his mother. Both he and Harry spent their formative years floating between various residences, as most Royals always have. But in their case it was because of the 'tug-of-love' battles between their parents. In the five years since the death of Princess Diana, William has become settled and looks forward to weekends and holidays. He has established a close relationship with

For their 1995 Christmas card, the Prince of Wales chose to place his sons in these large urns on either side of him as he sat on a stone bench in the garden at Highgrove. The little dog in the foreground just happened to be there and joined in.

Prince Charles, and together they enjoy walking in the gardens, riding, hunting during the season and even just sitting in the drawing room, talking over family problems, of which there have been far too many in recent months.

Camilla Parker Bowles is often seen at Highgrove or St James's Palace, and the boys have accepted her role in their father's life, albeit to different degrees. William is more cautious than Harry, and while he gets on well with Camilla generally, the relationship is said to be nowhere near as warm as has been suggested. He is friendly with her for his father's sake but William remembers his mother too well for him to accept any other woman as a replacement. In the early days following Diana's death, Camilla's visits to Highgrove were restricted to occasional afternoons for tea, when she would chat to William and Harry about school, sports and how they were getting on with their studies. The conversations were deliberately kept low-key and on 'safe' subjects. Prince Charles encouraged the contact as he was anxious for his children to establish good relations with the woman he loved. And Camilla never tried to push things along too fast. She also frequently brought her own children Tom and Laura, who had become, and remain, good friends with William.

When William left Eton his relationship with Camilla became strained for a while. He felt she was spending too much time at Highgrove and was trying to take over what had been his and his father's family home. He was right in a way as practically all traces of Diana's presence have been removed, and Camilla's influence is evident in every room except those belonging to William and Harry, where they have insisted that their own tastes and style should prevail. Harry was much more relaxed than William about Camilla's presence, but for a time William retreated into his shell once more, as he had immediately after Diana's death. The feeling didn't last long, only a matter of months, but Mrs Parker Bowles knew there was something wrong, and Prince Charles had to reassure his elder son that there was nothing to worry about. Nobody was going to force him out of his own home – or take the place of his late mother. William now keeps his own counsel about his feelings for Camilla, but he realizes that she is a permanent fixture in his father's life, and even if he did want to make an issue of the fact, he knows Prince Charles would not give way.

The ideal solution to the problem would, of course, be for William to move into a separate establishment. At twenty-one, he does not want to live under his father's roof for too much longer, and The Queen also understands his need for

Prince Charles with his long-time companion, Camilla Parker Bowles, visit Canisbay Church in Caithness during a summer holiday in 2002. They like to stay at the Queen Mother's former home Birkhall, which is in the process of being restored.

Opposite: *The crowds had waited for hours outside the parish church at Sandringham on Christmas Day 2001 to see the Royal Family and Prince William didn't disappoint them. He spent several minutes chatting among them and receiving bunches of flowers.*

Prince William

a house of his own. When William finishes his studies at university, he will choose a home. The Queen has already indicated that she is prepared to give him a house when he wants one and the idea of having his own place has great appeal. When Prince Charles moves across Stable Yard to Clarence House, his large apartment in York House will become vacant and this would be a suitable London home for his elder son. It would be perfect for him and an ideal choice from The Queen's point of view as it would keep him close to Buckingham Palace. If he does take it on he will also have to have a substantial domestic household to run it, but nowhere near the eighty-odd staff his father employs as he is unlikely to need the administrative and secretarial back-up Prince Charles requires. He is also going to want a country home for the weekends, but it is

thought that Gloucestershire may be too far from London and in any case too near the 'Royal Triangle' with Prince Charles, the Princess Royal and Prince and Princess Michael of Kent all within a few miles of each other. So somewhere in the home counties is thought to be a better option. Again, The Queen may come to the rescue with one of the grace and favour properties in or near Windsor.

Of course, William will have his own thoughts on the subject and may decide to buy a house himself. He has the money, and his trustees are believed to be sympathetic if he wants to spend some of the capital, but with an abundance of Royal residences in England and Scotland, some of which will almost certainly be looking for tenants in the not too distant future, he could be spoilt for choice.

At Home

ten University

If William had no say in choosing which school he attended, he was consulted about the choice of university (after a small committee had made their recommendations to his father), although Oxbridge was ruled out early on.

William *did* opt to join a Scottish university, but his preference might well have been the livelier Edinburgh rather than the smaller, but socially superior St Andrews, where he enrolled to read History of Art. Scotland's capital city has more temptations with its much larger student body and lively nightlife. Admitting that Edinburgh had been a possibility, William said it was 'too busy' for his liking. He added: 'In St Andrews it's a small community and so I can mingle how I like. Edinburgh is just too big and too busy.' William also disclosed that he did not want to go to an English university 'because I have lived there and wanted to get away and try somewhere else. I also knew I would be seeing a lot of Wales in the future.' Commenting on the social life of the university, he said 'Weekends at St Andrews, I've been told, are not particularly vibrant . . . I'm not a party animal, despite what people might think, but I like to go out sometimes like anyone else.' When he was asked what he was looking forward to most at university, he replied, 'I'm particularly looking forward to being able to manage my own time in a relaxed atmosphere. Having more independence is quite a big thing, although I've always got policemen around so I'm never completely independent.' Reports that the Prince frequently gives his protection officers the slip and enjoys a few hours of freedom without their presence are untrue. Not

one of them would obey him if he asked them to leave him alone. It would be more than their careers are worth.

However, St Andrews has not been an unqualified success. There were some doubts that he would continue after reports that he was bored at university during his first year, and saw no reason why he should remain. He would have preferred to spend the next few years in the armed forces, but with the world situation in a such a volatile state, and the prospect of conflict involving British forces never far away, there is no chance that The Queen would allow her grandson to be placed in a position where he might have to be prevented from going into active service in view of his future role. And if William did enter the Army, Navy or RAF, he would not accept any special privileges, or be prepared to take a back seat while his comrades went into action. Nor would his father want him to. Prince Andrew fought gallantly in the Falklands Campaign in 1982 as a helicopter pilot and his reputation, quite rightly, was enhanced immeasurably because of it. But William does not have that opportunity. Andrew is a second son, with very little prospect of ever succeeding to the throne; William is next but one in the line of succession. He probably will undergo some military training eventually, winning his pilot's wings and making a parachute jump, as his father did, but only after he has completed his education, and that means staying at St Andrews University.

When William's education after Eton was being discussed, a small, eclectic group of Prince Charles's friends, and others who might be able to make a contribution to the debate, were invited to meet at St James's Palace. Among them were the Bishop of London, one of Britain's most senior Army officers, Sir Charles (now Lord) Guthrie, and Chris Patten, a man who has held many high-profile positions in public life, including several ministerial and Cabinet appointments. His place in history is guaranteed by virtue of the fact that he was Britain's last Governor of Hong Kong and many people will remember the pictures of him carrying the Union flag under his arm as he boarded the Royal Yacht *Britannia* to be carried away from the former colony in 1997. Today he is one of Britain's two European Commissioners, with responsibility for external

Previous page: *Prince William wears the regulation 'uniform' of jeans and sweater as he walks through the campus with the Prince of Wales during his introduction to St Andrews University in September 2001.*

Chris Patten, the last Governor of Hong Kong and at present one of Britain's two European Commissioners, was consulted about William's gap year and university plans.

affairs. The other Commissioner is Neil Kinnock. Chris Patten explained what happened at that meeting with the Prince of Wales:

> In the first place I was slightly surprised to be asked as I did not know Prince William, even though I had been friendly with Prince Charles for some years, mainly through our mutual interest in education when I was Minister in that department and later when I was Secretary of State for the Environment. Also I am Chancellor of Newcastle University, so, presumably that was the reason I was asked. [He was also elected Chancellor of Oxford University in March 2003.] We met in St James's Palace and had a very congenial lunch hosted by the Prince of Wales, with every item on the menu an organic product of his home farm at Highgrove. Then we got down to business under the chairmanship of Prince Charles who was clearly concerned that he

should be in the best possible position to offer good advice to his son. He was determined that decisions, however well intentioned, would not be imposed on Prince William without his agreement and due consideration of his own interests and ambitions. And, of course, we were all aware that Prince William was in a unique position and was not, and never would be, in the same position as other young men of his age.

The discussion was divided into two parts: the first to examine what he might do in his gap year and the second to see which university he might attend and the sort of courses that might interest him. It was a wide-reaching brief and one that attracted serious discussion.

When the subject arose of William going to university – and this debate took place before his A-level results were known – again a number of criteria were considered, as Chris Patten reveals:

First, it was important that his own interests, and not necessarily just his academic qualifications, were taken into account. Then, because of his position, there was the whole question of finding somewhere where he could enjoy a certain amount of privacy. So when we put all these points together a small number of universities suggested themselves, with St Andrews emerging as the front runner, and I think it turned out to be an excellent choice. At the time I had no idea of his intellectual abilities, but generally the opinion seemed to be that Oxford and Cambridge were ruled out. To get there today one has to be confident of three A grades, and even then, with the climate at many colleges being to prefer taking students from the state sector rather than public schools, it is extremely difficult to obtain a place. So when you think of the amount of publicity there would have been if he had tried for Oxbridge I think it was sensible for it not to be considered.

Prince William is the most high-profile student St Andrews University has enrolled to date and I asked Mr Patten, as a chancellor of a university himself, what effect this might have had:

I think it probably meant an increase in applications for a couple of years and certainly a large increase in interest from the United States resulting from the publicity. But I doubt whether the impact has been all that profound because universities are pretty self-confident institutions and young people are incredibly good at taking people in their stride. And I think that after the first explosion of media attention, the students would have treated William just as they do anyone else. Because of my own loyalties I would have liked him to come to Newcastle, but I realize it would have been more difficult to manage the media side of things than it is at St Andrews. They are a comparatively small university, slightly off the beaten track, and I'm sure it was the right decision for William to go there.'

So, St Andrews it was. Nestled in the Scottish countryside, just 55 miles from Edinburgh, with a 6,000-strong student body – 10 per cent of whom are from the USA – William has since said 'It has a real community feel to it.' This is because St Andrews is not a campus university, but one integrated with the city and its 16,000 inhabitants. Founded in 1411, it is Scotland's oldest university and the third oldest in the United Kingdom. However, before he was allowed to take up residence in the town, William's grandmother, The Queen, laid down certain rules. They were: no smoking, only moderate drinking and definitely no drugs; if he went out with a girl, he was not to be seen kissing her in public; never to try to get rid of his official Royal Protection Department bodyguard, even at private parties; and never to discuss any member of the Royal Family with anyone, including those with whom he became close. This last was totally unnecessary, for ever since he was a child, William had had instilled in him a deep suspicion of strangers. Even when he was at prep school, he never relaxed sufficiently to be caught off guard – by either his fellow pupils or, more dangerously, their parents.

In an interview he gave shortly before leaving for St Andrews, William revealed how 'streetwise' he was when said he knew some people would try to cultivate him because of who he was, adding, 'but I'm not that stupid'.

The university authorities are reluctant to discuss any aspect of William's life but admit that there was an immediate and significant increase in the number of applications from would-be undergraduates, particularly female candidates. And residents of the town are clearly delighted to have such a well-known student staying among them. Local businesses have benefited considerably with a huge influx of visitors to the town and property prices have skyrocketed since William arrived.

University

Both William and Harry are excellent polo players, but Harry is said to possess the more natural talent. Both are seen here at Cirencester Park Polo Club in 2001, just before William went to university.

The townspeople are fiercely protective of the Prince's privacy and visiting journalists encounter a blank wall of silence when they try to obtain information about William's whereabouts, who his friends are and where he spends his off-duty hours. When he arrived in the town he was given a warm welcome, but the locals realized he wanted to be left alone and they have done just that. If he is seen around he will usually say good morning or acknowledge familiar faces in some way but the townsfolk know he appreciates the way they respect his need to be treated like any other student.

The university introduces first-year students to their new way of life by appointing a group of older students to advise them. Among William's 'parents' were his 'mother' Alice Drummond-Hay, from Connecticut, USA, who happens to be the granddaughter of the Earl of Crawford and Bacarres, a former senior member of the Queen Mother's household, while his 'father' was Gus McMyn, like William, an old Etonian. St Andrews claims it does not involve itself in choosing the young men and women who take on these responsibilities, and the Palace also denies indicating any preference. But it seems hardly credible that these two people were not hand-picked.

A 22-year-old fellow student was Elizabeth Hadley from Preston in Lancashire. After graduating, she moved to New Zealand where she lives in Auckland, and from there she spoke about her final year at St Andrews when she lived in the same student residence as William: 'I went out one night with one of my university "children". She was only eighteen and had a bit too much to drink and was sick afterwards. She was living in a different hall and didn't know Will but when I took her back to our place she saw him and I introduced them. She is a gorgeous 5 ft 10 in girl with long blonde hair and was absolutely gobsmacked when she met him. She shook his hand and next morning said, "Oh my God, I met Prince William and I had sick in my hair and sick on my hand – and I shook his hand." She was mortified.' Lizzie, as she prefers to be known, recalled that he tended to associate with the more aristocratic students, the 'Yahs' as the rest of the student body called them. She continues: 'The genuine "Yahs" were fine, all products of their upbringing, with perfect manners. They also had better clothes than the rest of us. The "Wannabe Yahs" were easy to spot with their fake pashminas and streaky hair. . . . Girls did get dressed up and hang about outside his lectures. But he never bothers with them. His own friends, some from his school days, both girls and guys, always surround him. If he had wanted to have a relationship, I'm sure he would have done.'

Lizzie says there is no truth in the stories that William is lonely and unhappy. According to her, he enjoys student life, likes going out and can often be found sitting on the staircase at night swapping jokes and chatting: 'He's just a nice normal very good-looking person who wants to get on with his studies. I didn't see any sign that he was having problems. Nobody is mean to him. He also wears the standard clothes for "Yahs": shirt with the collar always turned up, sweater, jeans and trainers.' One of the girls 'accidentally' brushed against William one day and rushed back to tell her friends that his sweater was pure cashmere. They said, "What do you expect? He is going to be a king one day."'

It also surprised some of William's colleagues that he did not stick to his own room all the time. He is a big fan of the TV soap operas – just like his mother – with *EastEnders* a particular favourite – and he preferred to watch in the communal area with the others, rather than in the privacy of his own study, even though he did have his own television set. William had quite a lot of baggage with him and at the end of each term all was loaded into two large Ford Galaxy people carriers. He left nothing behind. And at the Valedictorian Dinner, a traditionally formal affair, he wore a dark lounge suit, rather than a dinner jacket or kilt.

On Sundays Lizzie used to read the tabloids, and William, who would not be seen buying them himself, often asked her to save them for him to read when she had finished. 'He always turned straight to the back pages to read the football stories, if there were any, and if there were any Royal stories that might have affected him he never showed it. It's the way he's been brought up.'

Lizzie said her friendship with the Prince came about through a note pushed underneath his door, and it wasn't even written by her, she was just delivering it:

I did it subtly because I didn't want anyone to think I was passing him a romantic message or anything like that. The note was actually from one of my friends who was on the water polo team, and it was reminding Will to come along. I wasn't too sure if he had received it so I went up and asked him. I'd just been out to the supermarket and my friend was standing behind me carrying a whole lot of toilet rolls with 'Touch Me' printed on them. It was a bit embarrassing as it was the first time I had met him. He was very polite and friendly, but a little guarded. He asked me if I played water polo and I said, 'No, I'm not exactly what you'd call aqua-dynamic.' He laughed at that.

Lizzie and William were staying at St Salvator's hall of residence at St Andrews, called 'Sallies' by the students. It is a rambling, Gothic co-ed student residence with male and females living on separate floors. Lizzie was on the floor below William and saw him often. She says, 'He used to talk about his brother Harry quite a lot and occasionally about his father, but never, ever about The Queen.'

The Prince surprised everyone when he refused to join one of the most elite social clubs in the university, as Lizzie reveals:

It's the Katherine Kennedy Club and is reserved for male students only. We all thought he would join but he didn't. He was friendly to everyone but only got close to a few after he was sure of them. He would invite a couple of

The Prince of Wales and Prince William of Wales arriving for a Golden Jubilee service at St Mary's Church in Swansea on 6 July 2002. This was one of several services they attended to mark the fiftieth anniversary of The Queen's accession, though, as William was still in his first year at university, he did not undertake too many official engagements.

friends to his room for a drink, but he could suss out those who were not genuine. He always said, 'Hi Lizzie' and asked how things were going, and one morning I was still half asleep and raced down to breakfast, squeezing into a tiny space on the bench, groaning and moaning. It was only after a few seconds that I realized I was squashing Will. But he's such a nice guy he just carried on chatting.

But William did not allow anyone to take liberties. One night in a popular student bar, a girl – for a dare – pinched his bottom. But she did not get the reaction she was hoping for. 'He turned around and gave her a scathing look, and she felt like a real fool,' says Lizzie. His friends were also very protective if visitors to the town tried to snatch photographs of him. They would sometimes even place their hands over the camera lens.

St Andrews is justly proud of having a Royal student and it has helped the economy of the town enormously in some ways. But for the other students there have also been certain drawbacks. Examination results are no longer posted on university notice boards and one café has been closed because it had access to the student records area. 'Some students were not happy about it, but that's the way it has had to be,' says Lizzie. Extra security cameras have been installed on the campus and, of course, the students have all become aware of the ever-present Royal protection officers who shadow William wherever he goes. What is normal procedure for him and an accepted part of his everyday life, takes a little getting used to by others who are more accustomed to a free and easy existence.

After living in hall for two years, William decided it was time to move out, and again this meant massive preparations. It was not simply a case of finding somewhere suitable and moving in. His security officers had to vet the place, which is near the town centre, and also check the background of the three other students who were going to share with him. They then needed to talk to William's new neighbours to see if there were any serious objections to his presence because of possible disruption to their lives, and with the local police and emergency services, making sure his flat was not too far away from their depots. However, contrary to some reports, the extra measures did not involve a great increase in costs. The security equipment that had been installed when he arrived at St Andrews – said to have cost about £100,000 – was simply moved out of St Salvator's and set up in and around his new apartment.

The move has meant William is more relaxed in his new surroundings, without constantly having to be on the look out for visitors who want to see him and, even more irritatingly, photograph him. It also means The Queen and Prince Charles can be satisfied that he has settled down at last to continue his studies, without showing any of the frustration he displayed during his first year.

So, in spite of the initial disappointment felt by William when he arrived at St Andrews, it looks very much as if it was a good choice after all – both for him and the university.

eleven
Wills and
Gran-Gran

William's great-grandmother, Queen Elizabeth the Queen Mother, who he always called Gran-Gran (his maternal grandmother, Frances Shand Kydd, was Supergran), was well known for her love of champagne, as well as gin and Dubonnet. She regarded champagne as medicinal and practically non-alcoholic and rarely a day passed without the odd glass or two.

One afternoon when William was visiting her at Clarence House, she was, as usual, having a glass of her favourite vintage and he asked if he might have a sip 'just to see what it tastes like'. At the time he was well below the legal age for drinking but she knew it would not do him any harm and she said of course he could, 'as long as you don't tell your father'. She knew that Prince Charles did not share her liberal views on under-age drinking, and would have been horrified if he had known, even though when he was just fourteen and still a pupil at Gordonstoun, he was once found having a sly cherry brandy in a local pub when he tried to escape a gang of reporters and photographers.

William discovered that indeed he did like the taste (unlike The Queen who rarely drinks the stuff) but on reaching the age of legal drinking, decided that he would keep to something more suitable to his age group. Most of his contemporaries at university do like champagne when it is on offer, but beer is more generally drunk (straight from the bottle, to avoid the possibility of someone 'spiking' the drink) along with some of the more exotic cocktails.

The ten-year-old Prince William offers to help his great-grandmother the Queen Mother up the steps of the Deanery at Windsor Castle as she leaves St George's Chapel after the Easter service in 1992.

Opposite: *Another Royal christening and the Queen Mother holds the baby William Arthur Philip Louis on her lap. It was an occasion for double celebration as the date of the christening – 4 August – also happened to be the Queen Mother's eighty-second birthday.*

Queen Elizabeth once said she could not understand the attraction of drinking something that had to have 'toys, fruit and umbrellas' in the glass.

The Queen Mother began thinking of both William's and Harry's future drinking from the moment they were born. She gave each of them a unique christening gift of a 'pipe' of vintage port, laid down at the cellars of the Royal wine merchants and increasing in value every year. A 'pipe' contains approximately 600 bottles and when William was born his was worth about £6,000. At the age of twenty-one, his pipe has increased in value to some £30,000, and that is without the special Royal association. These were marvellous presents indeed.

Another incident concerning William and his great-grandmother also involved champagne. They were both staying at Sandringham at the time when Her Majesty was being ferried around the estate in her famous golf buggy, painted in her racing colours of blue and gold. She was famous for urging her liveried chauffeur to 'go faster' all the time, as even at ninety-eight years old she still loved the thrill of speed. One day William cheekily challenged her to a race, suggesting a magnum of champagne for the winner. But his great-grandmother reluctantly declined, knowing that her daughter, The Queen, would not be amused if she found out – as she always did. But secretly she was delighted at the prospect, and said that if she had been a couple of years younger she would have accepted – and no doubt won.

The relationship between the Queen Mother and Prince William and Prince Harry was very special. She told the rest of the family that they helped to keep

her young. And once when Prince Charles, who was always solicitous of her welfare, told the boys off for giving her what he thought were far too boisterous hugs, she replied in no uncertain terms: 'Leave them alone. It's a long time since I had a nice cuddle from one handsome young man, never mind two.' That summed up the relationship perfectly. They had enormous respect for her but not in the reverential way of earlier generations. William in particular liked to joke with her and tell her about his latest escapades, including, in recent years, a few details about his social life and not leaving out the romantic interludes. She loved it. There was nothing he could not say to her and she enjoyed all the latest gossip. She was especially fascinated when it came to goings on at the

Palace, and he was never as inhibited as his father when it came to regaling her with tales of who was doing what with whom.

William and Harry's London home in St James's Palace is just 25 yd from Clarence House and the boys occasionally used to slip across to have tea with their great-grandmother. But not as often as has been sometimes suggested. Members of the Royal Family live remarkably separate lives and rarely do their paths cross unless it is on an official occasion or for a special family function. The Queen Mother's birthdays were always celebrated with every family member 'on parade'. But there were many times when they would go for months without seeing each other. In the latter years of her life, both Princes Charles and William tried to see her more frequently, and William never had the slightest trouble in talking to a woman more than five times his own age. He could tell her anything and could also get away with saying things that no one else – including The Queen – would have dared. The Queen was sometimes heard to remark, when another member of the family suggested something she was not too sure about, 'Oh! We'll have to see what Mummy thinks about that, but be very careful of the way you put it to her.'

The difference in height between William and his great-grandmother was another source of amusement to them both. At 6 ft 2 in and still growing, he was well over a foot taller than Queen Elizabeth, and once when they were having an official photograph taken he leaned over and said, 'We're like Little and Large.' They had to delay taking the picture until she stopped shaking with laughter.

Perhaps the basis for the relationship between the Queen Mother and William and Harry was that she was completely non-judgemental. She was not horrified at what she read in the newspapers; even when Harry was revealed as having smoked cannabis and been seen drinking while under-age, she was not at all shocked.

William has said that one of his greatest regrets is that he never had the opportunities that his father had to share some of the Queen Mother's favourite

Previous pages: *The Queen Mother often said she loved having young people around her and William claimed he could say anything at all to her. This photograph was taken on Her Majesty's ninety-fourth birthday.*

Prince William, already towering over his father at 6 ft 2 in, joins his brother and their great-grandmother as she prepares to meet the crowds outside Clarence House on 4 August 2001 – her 101st birthday.

Even at the age of a hundred the Queen Mother shows her independence by declining the helping hand of Prince Charles as she walks down the steps at St Paul's Cathedral followed by The Queen, Prince Philip, William and Harry and the Duke of York. They had been attending a service to mark her hundredth birthday.

pastimes. Prince Charles has often claimed that the best holidays he can remember involved 'standing up to my thighs in icy water, fishing in the River Dee in Scotland in the company of my grandmother'. William would have liked to do the same but by the time he was old enough to do it, his great-grandmother's active fishing days were over, so she could only watch from the riverbank through powerful binoculars.

Princes Charles and William and the latter's cousin, Zara Phillips, join the Queen Mother at Clarence House as she greets the wellwishers who have gathered to see her on her ninety-eighth birthday.

The Queen Mother's steward, William Tallon, bends over Princess Margaret, in a wheelchair, as the Queen Mother and the three princes look on. Four generations of royalty are present.

A solemn occasion as The Queen, the Prince of Wales, the Duke of Edinburgh, Prince Willliam, the Earl of Wessex, the Duke of York and Prince Harry attend the funeral of the Queen Mother at Westminster Abbey in April 2002.

Opposite: *Prince William and Prince Harry, in full, formal dress, arrive at St Paul's Cathedral on 11 July 2000 to attend a service celebrating the Queen Mother's hundredth birthday.*

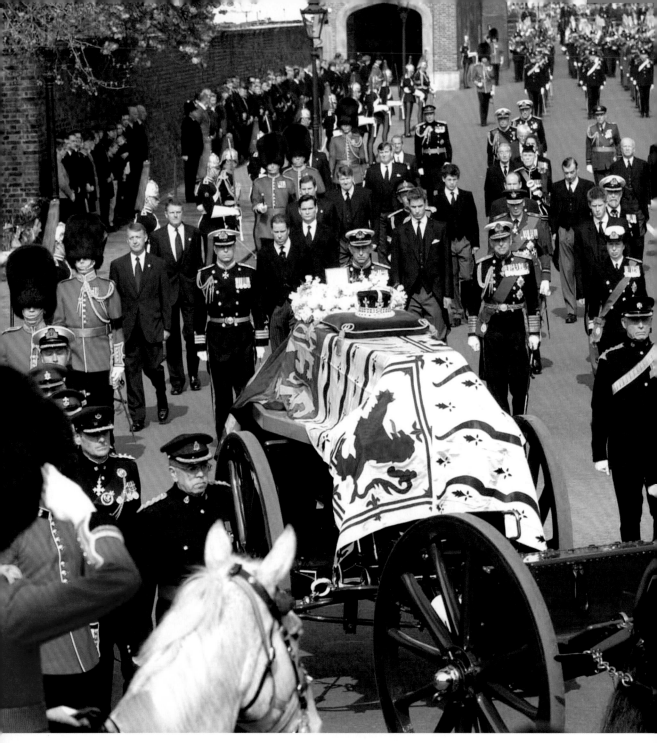

The male members of the Royal Family – and the Princess Royal in naval uniform – follow the Queen Mother's coffin, carried on a gun carriage, en route to Westminster Abbey for the funeral service.

When Charles and Diana's marriage broke up, the Queen Mother's first thoughts were for their children. She realized how traumatic the after-effects could be at such a vulnerable age and paid them particular attention. When they were about to move from their family home at Kensington Palace, after the death of their mother, it was she who suggested that they should move lock, stock and barrel, taking all their favourite bits of furniture with them, so the change would not be too much of a shock. Prince Charles agreed, even down to lifting the carpets from their old rooms and laying them in their new quarters in St James's Palace. It was a shrewd and compassionate thought on the part of the Queen Mother and one that was later much appreciated by her great-grandsons.

The boys were naturally deeply saddened when they were told of the Queen Mother's death. They were on holiday in Switzerland with their father and immediately flew back to Britain. It was the first and only time that Prince Charles and his sons were allowed to fly together in the same aircraft, and even in this emergency, the permission of The Queen had to be given before the flight could take place.

The Queen Mother gave the appearance of being a soft woman but that outward shell concealed an inner toughness and she knew that to survive William and Harry would need more than a little of that same quality. So she wasn't a shoulder to cry on, more a steadying influence and just someone who was there when she was needed. William recognized straight away the value of having someone like his great-grandmother, who had been through so many trying times herself, to unburden himself to when he felt the need.

Prince William insisted on walking in the funeral procession of his great-grandmother, Queen Elizabeth the Queen Mother. He was determined to pay a final tribute to the woman he admired and respected almost above all others.

William has inherited many of the characteristics of the Queen Mother including being able to separate his personal life from the official face he is required to present when on show to the public. All the Royals learn the art from an early age. When Princess Anne is with her tiny circle of really close friends – and they can be counted on the fingers of both hands – she is relaxed, a brilliant conversationalist and does not stand on ceremony. It is a complete contrast to her image when she is on duty. Then she is totally professional, gives the impression that she is never fully relaxed, always watching to see that nobody gets too close, and no one would dream of treating her with any degree of informality.

William has already learned some of these skills, but with the common touch allied to the undoubted star quality that he has inherited from his mother and great-grandmother. It is a formidable combination and one on which he will come to rely more and more in the years to come. They are also the kind of attributes he may be looking for in a future wife. A woman who looks like his mother with the character of Gran-Gran.

twelve
The Sporting *Prince*

On his eighteenth birthday, Prince William was given the present he cherishes above all others, even the VW Golf car he later received. His father gave him a hand-made twelve-bore shotgun costing over £20,000. But it was not the price that made it so valuable in William's eyes, but the fact that he could now indulge in his favourite sport, shooting, with his own weapon and not one that had been borrowed.

William likes to try his hand at everything and here he is seen on a canoeing holiday at White Sands Bay at St David's, West Wales, in 1999.

William has always enjoyed speed and even as a young boy he couldn't resist driving a go-kart at the British Grand Prix meeting in 1988.

Opposite: *William cannot remember when he could not ride and even before he was seven years old he was competing. Here he is led over a small jump at Minchinhampton Horse Trials in May 1989.*

Although the young Prince had always shown an aptitude for different sports – water polo, swimming, riding, soccer and rugby – shooting quickly became a passion that shows no sign of diminishing. He will go anywhere for a day's sport – Sandringham, Balmoral, Highgrove – and he particularly enjoys crossing the fields to the Princess Royal's estate at Gatcombe, where she often holds shooting weekends.

William also likes to spend a few days in the company of the Duke and Duchess of Westminster (she, of course, is his godmother) on their 14,000-acre estate at Abbeystead in Lancashire. There are plenty of country houses with enough land to hold shooting parties, and as one of William's friends, who has been at several of these affairs, once remarked, 'Just like his grandfather, Prince Philip, he'll shoot anything that moves.' His enthusiasm for the sport knows no limits and in this he is encouraged by The Queen and Prince Philip, both of whom grew up immersed in this particular field sport. The Queen is an excellent shot but, like most ladies, sticks to 'picking up' while the men do the actual shooting. At Sandringham, Prince Philip holds the record for killing several thousand birds in a single day – and none of his guests is prepared to challenge him.

Princess Diana hated anything to do with guns and she tried, unsuccessfully, to persuade both her sons not to take up shooting. When William was a little boy his mother told him how cruel it was to kill any living creature for pleasure. But hers was a lone voice among the Royal Family. Even Princess Margaret and the Queen Mother, neither of whom lifted a gun in their lives, believed it was perfectly natural for all men to shoot and encouraged their grandchildren to take it up.

The Royal Family are extremely competitive with each other when it comes to sporting activities and they also take great pride when one of their number achieves success. So it is not surprising that William holds his aunt, the Princess Royal, in great esteem and considers her brilliance as a horsewoman to be a wonderful achievement. She was an Olympic competitor in Montreal in

Opposite: *William's physical courage has never been in doubt. He is an enthusiastic horseman and thoroughly enjoys the rough and tumble of polo. He is seen here in action at the Beaufort Club in July 2002.*

Right: *Prince Charles believes you cannot start too young, so he was delighted when eight-year-old William took an early interest in polo. He is seen here at Cirencester Park Polo Club in June 1990.*

1976, and won the European Three-Day Event Championship in 1971, when she was also voted the BBC Sportswoman of the Year. She has encouraged her nephew in his riding and occasionally invites him to try some of the more difficult event courses. He shows no fear and is a natural horseman, though some say he is not in quite the same class as his brother Harry. And just like his aunt, he likes a course to be demanding. In fact the tougher the better. It's as if he is always trying to prove something to himself. He enjoys hunting but not with the same enthusiasm as Harry, who loves the thrill of the chase. William says that there is too much hanging around at most hunts, even though he enjoys it when a fox has been sighted and the pursuit is on.

Both brothers play polo with aggressive ability and an enthusiasm that is shared by their father and grandfather. With polo, William adopts the same attitude he shows towards all the other sports he enjoys. He has to be a winner. The old Olympic ideal that it is the taking part that counts, not the winning, cuts no ice with him. He likes to be first, so when he decided to take up polo, his father employed one of the world's finest Argentinian instructors to give him tuition. And even though he has now been playing for several years, William still has lessons frequently. His physical courage has never been in doubt. He has had many falls playing polo and also, when coming up against better players, numerous encounters in which he has come off worst. But it has not put him off the game, indeed, the more physical it gets, the better he seems to like it.

But shooting is the great love of William's life. He was first allowed to join in the family shoots – as a spectator – when he was just eight years old. His father had him measured for his first set of shooting clothes and the boy was thrilled to be allowed to join the rest of the party at their traditional breakfast before going out into the fields. And just like any true lover of field sports, the weather did not bother him one bit. He would enjoy it just as much in the rain, snow or hail as when the sun was shining. The Queen was once asked why she enjoyed trooping through the fields in all winds and weathers. She did not bother to answer because she thought the question stupid and unnecessary. She was also asked what would happen if it was pouring down with rain. 'We get wet' was the reply.

The fact that Prince Charles was, and remains, an excellent shot has continued to be a source of great pride to William. He has always taken enormous pleasure in his father's success with a gun, as he did when Charles was a regular polo player.

William had known from an early age that his mother disapproved, but he only learned quite how much she hated guns and anything to do with them during the shoots at Sandringham. The catering arrangements on these occasions are carried out with as much attention to detail as any other Royal function. Lunch is taken in a village hall on the estate and picnic snacks are available while the shooters are still in the field. They do not like to waste time by trooping back to the main house for meals. But these picnic lunches are not like any most people enjoy. Everything is of the very best quality: food, wine, tea and coffee are brought from Sandringham and laid out by liveried footmen with the finest china, crystal and cutlery being used. Most days The Queen and other guests who are not shooting will join the men for a bite to eat and a glass or two of wine, and William, before he got the message, often tried to persuade his mother to join them as well. After a couple of reluctant appearances, just to please him, she always declined. Not even the presence of The Queen and Prince Philip could make her change her mind as she thought that if she did turn up, it might be taken as a sign that she approved of the killing, even tacitly. William quickly learned that there was no chance of his mother ever taking up the sport he loved and they agreed not to mention it too often, as it frequently meant one of them would be upset.

And if there is one sport that Diana would certainly have hated her sons to take part in, it would be deer hunting. At Balmoral, William loves to spend hours in the wet heather, stalking the older deer that the gamekeepers have decided must be culled that season. It is nothing for him to stay out for six or seven hours at a time, up hill and down dale, before reaching the point where the target can be safely shot. You need to be ultra fit and have endless patience for deer stalking and William does not look for any other entertainments after a day on the hills. A hot bath, a good dinner with the odd beer or two thrown in and an early night are all he wants in order to be ready for the next day's sport. Diana would never have consented to her sons taking part in what she regarded

Prince Charles persuaded William to pose for the cameras before they took to the slopes during their skiing holiday in Klosters, Switzerland, in 2002. William still doesn't like having his photograph taken but now accepts it is all part of being royal.

Opposite: *William was ten years old when his father took him skiing in Canada and was already up to Prince Charles's shoulder. His natural sense of balance has made him an excellent all-round sportsman, but Prince Harry claims to be the better skier.*

Right: *A relaxed and happy William enjoying the snow in Canada in 1997. It is one of his favourite countries and he always enjoys his visits, particularly when there is the opportunity to ski.*

as a barbaric practice. She thought it was bad enough to kill pheasants, grouse and even vermin such as foxes. But deer were definitely off-limits.

It was when William reached his twelfth birthday that he was allowed to join his father and grandfather stalking. He had been given excellent tuition in handling a light 28-bore shotgun so he was never nervous about entering what was, for him, the 'big time'. He had also watched for years the way the gun dogs had worked, picking up the birds once they had fallen and he admired the professionalism of the loaders who kept the guns ready at all times. Prince Charles sends his valets to Purdey or Holland & Holland where they are given a short course in loading shotguns. They are also measured for special suits of clothing to be worn in the field. Officially, the loaders are all volunteers and the Royal Family does not force them to take on this duty if they object. But so far

Prince William and the Prince of Wales applauding the winners at the Beaufort Polo Club, 2002. Prince Charles is thrilled that both his sons have inherited his passion for the sport.

Opposite: *One of the reasons for William's success at Eton was his sporting prowess. He played rugby for the school's 2nd XV until a hand injury prevented him from carrying on and on the soccer field captained his house. Here he is seen playing in an inter-house tournament in June 2000.*

none has expressed any dislike of the task. In fact, most of them thoroughly enjoy a couple of days in the open air.

Another sport that William enjoys but again one his mother disliked is fishing. He was taught fly-fishing by his father on the River Dee in Scotland and often spent hours in the company of his great-grandmother, Queen Elizabeth the Queen Mother. She never lost her love of it so was delighted when William showed an aptitude for fishing. He says one of the great attractions is the solitude, 'Apart from the sport, I find it is also a great time for thinking.'

Prince Charles has always loved to ski and most winters he can be found on the slopes in one of the more fashionable European resorts. William and Harry often join their father, reluctantly agreeing to the, by now, obligatory photo-call before they set off for their day on the slopes. Charles thinks they have reached an understanding with the press but William does not agree. He hates the paparazzi, in particular those freelance European photographers who make a living by taking pictures of celebrities in unguarded moments, and knows they will never leave him alone. So last year he refused to accompany his father to Klosters. Charles was naturally very disappointed, but nothing he could do or say would make William change his mind, although it meant denying himself another of his favourite pastimes.

At Eton, William enjoyed being a 'wet-bob', as those who row are called. The only problem was that as soon as any of the local girls heard that he was on the River Thames, they flocked to the riverside, calling out to him and generally making his life pretty miserable. His friends at the school tried to protect him from this unwanted attention, but they were not always successful and he did not go out as often as he would have wished.

Many in the Royal Family prefer animals to people and William is no exception. He loves having dogs around the place, especially when he goes for solitary walks in the gardens at Highgrove or the grounds at Sandringham and Balmoral. He can often be seen surrounded by black Labradors on one of The Queen's estates and when he is in the company of his cousins Peter and Zara Phillips the conversation is as likely as not to turn to sport. Peter has always been something of a hero figure, mainly because he represented Scotland at junior level when he played rugby, and Zara is following in her mother's footsteps in her equestrian career. But so far, William has shown no great inclination to take his sporting activities to a higher level. He knows it would attract even more attention of the sort he detests if he were to achieve international status in any of his chosen activities.

One of his contemporaries at Eton, who has since joined him at St Andrews, says of William's sporting prowess, 'He is totally without fear. If he has one fault, it is that he jumps in without thinking about the consequences. If he wasn't as well-built as he is, he could easily have suffered a serious injury by now. But he has perfect balance, and that, combined with a powerful physique, means he can play any contact sport – rugby or soccer – and give as good as he gets. He is a natural leader, and I have to say, he loves being captain of any team he plays in. He is not so good at taking orders.'

thirteen
A Most Eligible *Bachelor*

'William's apparent shyness is just a cover. There's no real nervousness at all, it's all a carefully and discreetly cultivated mannerism to make people, girls especially, fall for him – and boy does it work.' An unusually astute insight to his character by a fellow student at St Andrews University who regularly sees him at parties.

Prince William has already inherited one of his father's titles, that of being the most eligible bachelor in the world. It is not a title he has sought but it is one of which he is secretly quite proud and when his brother Harry teases him about it, he may protest, but it's rather half-hearted.

Prince Charles carried the burden, if that is what it was, of being the young man every mother in the world wanted as a son-in-law, from the age of eighteen until he married Lady Diana Spencer, by which time he was thirty-two. He too enjoyed the focus of attention that accompanied the title and was never happier than when he was seen in the company of beautiful young women, whether they were candidates as future wives or not.

William has not yet got around to looking for prospective brides, but whenever he is seen at polo matches or other fashionable outings, there is usually a group of what used to be called debutantes hanging around. These days they are more likely to be the daughters of successful City stockbrokers with the odd aristocrat thrown in for good measure, but as long as they are presentable in his eyes, they are always welcome. He likes to be seen with

Prince William and the Prince of Wales, the latter the former 'most eligible bachelor', the other the present holder of the title, at a garden party in the grounds of the Palace of Holyroodhouse in Edinburgh, July 2002. This was one of the rare occasions when William was required to wear formal clothes; he usually carried his top hat rather than wear it.

attractive girls, just like his uncle Andrew, the Duke of York. William seems to prefer tall, slim women.

William was spared the embarrassment of having his father explain the facts of life to him. That lesson was taught at Eton, much to his and Prince Charles's relief. But it was Charles who tried to tell him about some of the predatory females he was likely to meet in his social life, sexual aggression being no longer the prerogative of eager young men. In Prince Charles's day as a single man, most of the young women he met would wait until the first moves were made by the male. These days the moves are just as likely to come from the adventurous girls who inhabit the social scene at all levels of society. Young people generally are more forward looking and open-minded than their parents were at the same age, and William is no exception. But he has told several of his friends that he is fully aware of the potential pitfalls waiting for him if he puts

William likes good-looking blonde-haired women and they don't come much more beautiful than supermodel Claudia Schiffer. Here they are together at Ashe Park in Hampshire after William's team had won the Porcelanosa Cup at a charity polo competition in 2002.

a foot wrong. The vast sums that newspapers and magazines are prepared to pay for 'kiss and tell' stories, particularly those involving The Queen's grandson, would tempt all but the ultra rich and very discreet.

William is by no means reticent when it comes to girls. He loves to party and chat up the best-looking girls in the room, and he knows that he can have virtually any of them simply by crooking his finger. He may not have marriage in mind and they are all equally aware that this would be highly improbable, but that does not stop any of them from enjoying flirting with the eventual heir to the throne and letting him know they are available if required.

One of William's Etonian friends who joined him at a party recently said afterwards, 'We were all having a marvellous time, dancing and drinking all over the place. I couldn't see Wills anywhere, then when I went into the kitchen, there he was surrounded by four or five gorgeous girls who were hanging on his every word. He was loving every minute of it – and so were they. He knew the effect

he was having, leaning back against the table edge holding a bottle of beer in his hand; like all of us he wouldn't dream of drinking out of a glass at a party. The girls couldn't get enough of him.'

Prince Charles encourages William to bring his friends, male and female, home to Highgrove whenever he likes, and to invite them to stay in his apartment at St James's Palace if they have been to a late party in London. He takes the sensible view that a more open attitude to his son's relationships will lessen the dangers. Both he and William know that when it comes to anything serious, the usual trawl through acceptable families will take place, and that any girl who is being considered as a wife will have to pass the

This exotic dancer has obviously caught William's attention as they chat – with his arm around her shoulders – in Edinburgh in 2001.

most rigorous vetting procedure. After the disastrous marriages of the Prince and Princess of Wales, the Duke and Duchess of York and, earlier, the first marriage of Princess Anne and Captain Mark Phillips, all of which ended in divorce, it is essential that the right partner is found for William. The Queen has already let it be known that she regards the choice of wife for Prince William to be of the utmost importance for the continuity of the monarchy.

In time William will inherit the titles his father now holds, together with the vast income from the Duchy of Cornwall. So eligible he may be, but when the time comes for him to marry, the choice may be severely limited. The disasters that have accompanied recent Royal marriages and suitably prospective partners becoming more reluctant to join the Royal Family, means he is going to have to be very lucky and selective when choosing a bride. The pool of European Royalty has all but dried up and the daughters of British aristocratic families no longer seem to be willing to be sacrificed on the altar of public service as they once were.

William himself has said that he is in no hurry, but it won't help if he delays as long as his father did. Prince Charles was thirty-two when he married the twenty-year-old Lady Diana Spencer, and she was one of very few young women who were acceptable. In other words with an unblemished past. Of course, it may well be that the example of his parents' marriage will cause William to hesitate before marrying. No one could blame him if that was the case, but The Queen and Prince Philip would like to see him settled before he is thirty. They believe the longer he delays the harder it will be in the end. And even though he himself may not be seriously looking for a spouse just yet, others in the Royal establishment are already taking soundings. At Buckingham Palace files are being prepared on prospective young women and a close watch is being kept to see if any of them emerges as a possible future princess – and queen. The Royal Household has an information network of families who have been known to Royalty for generations; this is how Lady Diana Spencer came to their attention. No moves will be made for some years to come, but if a possible candidate features in the gossip columns too frequently or is seen with unsuitable companions, she will quickly be struck off the list. The Queen and Prince Philip take a personal if distant interest in these preliminary moves with William, of course, being kept in total ignorance.

Whether Charles took the advice of the late Earl Mountbatten of Burma, the man he described as 'my honorary grandfather', to 'sow as many wild oats as

Prince William always makes time to meet the wellwishers who wait to see the Royal Family as they leave the parish church at Sandringham on Christmas Day, and he is seen doing this in 1998. It is now a tradition that posies of flowers are offered and he appreciates the affectionate gestures.

you can before you settle down to a steady marriage', has never been recorded. There is certainly very little evidence that he indulged in large numbers of love affairs. If he did, he must have been very fortunate in the choice of partners, for none has ever leaked her story to the media.

Charles has tried hard to instil in William the fact that duty must be paramount. It comes before personal happiness and private emotions. He has pointed out that The Queen has sacrificed much of her own family life for public service. William understands the demands that will be made on him, but the rebel in his personality sometimes makes him question the need for such self-sacrifice in a modern world. He sees the example of other European monarchies where successful marriages are made without the need for monarchical or political expediency, and wonders why, in Britain, it is still considered so vital for the heir to the throne to make a 'suitable' marriage just because the woman will one day be Queen. He has argued that he should be allowed to make his own choice, and that the family and the country should have enough confidence in his ability to make that choice without submitting various names to Palace and Government authorities for their approval. He is hardly likely to choose someone as unsuitable, for example, as the Duchess of York, whose unconventional behaviour at one time caused some embarrassment to the Royal Family. At the same time, William will not be forced to consider only the existing Royal Families of Europe where in generations past, cousins married cousins. When the time comes for him to choose a bride, she will be someone of his own age, perhaps someone he met at university or during his gap year, and maybe not even from a traditional aristocratic background. But her family will be thoroughly investigated, she herself will undergo the most stringent vetting and only when the Palace is satisfied that there are no skeletons in her cupboard, will an engagement be permitted. William already accepts these ground rules, even if privately he would prefer nothing of the sort to happen.

He enjoys the company of glamorous blonde-haired women and at St Andrews there is a wide selection of American beauties, most of whom come from extremely rich families who would be delighted if their daughter married into the House of Windsor.

The Queen's views on making the right choice have been strengthened by the revelations that emerged during and following the Paul Burrell trial. She and

Prince Charles were all too aware of the distress caused to William and Harry by the stories concerning their late mother in all their squalid detail. The boys, too, now understand the need for their future spouses to be not only women with the purest reputations, but also women who will not rock the boat once they have joined the Royal Family.

Prince Charles has discussed William's social life with his son many times, but it is highly unlikely that he would have raised the delicate topic of Wills's love life. Both would have been far too embarrassed to talk about it, and, anyway, Charles realizes that his elder son is far more advanced than he was at the same age, so to offer such advice would be both unnecessary and superfluous.

William only has to be observed with a young woman for them to be linked together, but three years ago, when he was eighteen, he dismissed rumours that he was dating the singer Britney Spears as 'nonsense'. Some of his friends said he was not too displeased at the suggestion, however, and perhaps it was just wishful thinking on his part. Others claimed it was a publicity stunt, not originated by him. Fiercely protective of his privacy, William has plenty of friends and acquaintances who happen to be girls, but so far there is no one with a special claim on his affections.

William has been seen in the company of a number of girls, some he has met on the polo circuit, others at St Andrews and a few introduced by his father. What is surprising is that so little is known about any of them. There is no conclusive evidence that any of these girls were at any time William's girlfriends. He has managed with remarkable efficiency to keep his relationships secret so far. Perhaps the fact that his dates all tend to be in 'safe houses' such as the cottage on the Balmoral Estate, The Queen has given him, or at the homes of the parents of the girls he is going out with, or at his apartment in St James's Palace, or even better, at Highgrove, where Prince Charles provides total security and privacy. He would love to take a girl out to dinner or for a drink, but he knows that within minutes crowds would gather and the media would be alerted. In addition there would have to be the ever-present police bodyguard in attendance. So a romantic evening is not the easiest thing to arrange.

Opposite: *Claudia Schiffer was among the guests at a party at Highgrove held in August 2001 to celebrate the installation of an Islamic garden designed for the Chelsea Flower Show and Prince William is enchanted.*

Davina Duckworth-Chad was one of the young women William invited to join him on a cruise through the Greek Isles in 1999. Her father is a former High Sheriff of Norfolk and she is a regular member of the Prince's inner circle.

Another friend of William's is Natalie Hicks Lobbecke whose name has been linked with his and who is often seen at polo matches around the country, including the fashionable Beaufort Polo Club where William regularly plays in the season.

The young women whose names have been linked with William read like a Who's Who of society and the aristocracy. Before starting university, he was seen in the company of Arabella Musgrave, whose father manages Cirencester Park Polo Club. In 1999, he was joined on a cruise through the Greek isles by several young women including Davina Duckworth-Chad, whose brother, James, is Equerry to The Queen and whose father is a former High Sheriff of Norfolk, where he owns a 2,000-acre estate. Emma Parker Bowles, Camilla's niece, is another girl said to be friendly with the Prince, as is Jonathan Aitken's daughter Victoria. The Knatchbulls have been associated with Royalty for generations through being part of the Mountbatten family. So it is no surprise to find Alexandra Knatchbull's name on the list of prospective girlfriends. Her father is Lord Romsey, Earl Mountbatten's grandson and one of William's godfathers, while Princess Diana was Alexandra's godmother. She, like the others, has never admitted to being a special companion, only good friends.

Perhaps William believes there is strength in numbers, because there has not been one single name that has emerged to eclipse the others in the list. Lady Katherine Howard, daughter of the Earl of Suffolk, has been linked with the eventual heir to the throne, but so too has society girl Emilia d'Erlanger. She is a fellow student at St Andrews, studying the same subject as William, and she was another of the special group invited to join him and Prince Charles on the Greek isles holiday, which was dubbed the 'Love Boat' cruise by the tabloids.

There are probably another dozen or so girls who could find themselves linked to William, and in some cases, they are young women who might have met him only once, if at all. But there is one something they all have in common. They are fiercely protective about William and he has been extraordinarily lucky to find so many girls with discretion prominent among their other undoubted qualities. They also seem to share similar looks.

Those who get to know the Prince well soon learn his favourite food and drinks. He likes salads, pasta and venison and he says he can eat chocolate in any form: as ice cream, in puddings or sauces. He is not a big drinker but he does enjoy beer, red wine and still water. The Prince William 'in crowd' also know he likes going to the cinema, which he is able to do with reasonable anonymity, and prefers action movies to those with too much talking. Ever since his mother first took him to Cardiff to watch Wales play rugby, he has continued

The three princes on the balcony of Buckingham Palace when they joined the rest of the Royal Family to help celebrate the hundredth birthday of the Queen Mother, August 2000.

to love the game and follows all the international matches. In this he has a close relation with a similar passion, as his aunt, the Princess Royal, is Patron of the Scottish Rugby Union, and never misses one of their games, at home or abroad, if she can help it. When Wales plays Scotland, they have a friendly rivalry that occasionally gets a little heated, but they are both delighted when either of their teams beats England.

William's clothes tend to be on the casual side, like most young people his age. But he does have a wardrobe with a number of formal suits, including dinner jackets and full evening and morning tails, which he is required to wear when he accompanies The Queen or his father to a public function. An unusual Christmas present from his father to the twenty-year-old Prince in 2002 was a black silk top hat costing £1,200. When he first had suits made to measure, apart from his Eton uniforms, he used his father's tailors in Savile Row, Anderson & Shepeard. These days he is more likely to patronize Turnbull & Asser in Jermyn Street, who not only make suits but also his and Prince Charles's shirts. Though, just like his father, William does not have to suffer the inconvenience of going into their premises in person. Instead, bolts of cloth are delivered to St James's Palace and he makes his choice. His measurements are taken, with any special requirements, such as, does he like double cuffs to show off his cuff-links? Yes, he does. He has a collection of gold and silver cuff-links, some given by his father and a special pair, a gift from Prince Philip. Does he like a wide 'cut-away' collar or one with a deep turn back, and for sports shirts and less formal wear, does he prefer the button-down collar favoured initially by 'Ivy-league' Americans and now more commonly by young people in the City. He does. William is nothing if not fashion conscious, and the finished garments are delivered to the Palace by one of Turnbull & Asser's most trusted assistants. His shoes are made by the Royal boot makers, Lobb & Co. in St James's, who have lasts of his feet, as they have of every male member of the Royal Family. Their shoes start at about £600 a pair, but with a fortune rumoured to amount to some £17 million already in the bank, the cost is not a major consideration.

In 1996 the American magazine *People* voted him the best-dressed teenager in the world, and he was modest enough to admit that if this was true it was all due to his father's senior valet Lee Dobson, who looks after his clothes when he is at home. In 2002, Prince Harry was voted the 'best date' by *Tatler* magazine, so he is fast catching up in the 'eligible bachelor' stakes.

William's circle of friends include boys he grew up with at Eton, girls who are at St Andrews and a wider group who are the children of friends of his father. But there's little doubt that he is closer to his Royal cousins than to anyone outside. The Princess Royal's children, Peter and Zara Phillips, are the closest of all. They live just a couple of miles from Highgrove and see a great deal of William and Harry. At the wedding reception for the Earl and Countess of Wessex, William, Harry, Peter and Zara, together with the children of the Duke of Gloucester and Prince and Princess Michael of Kent, shared a table which was the most boisterous in the room. Zara loves to tease William; she knows exactly how to make him blush and she can get away with saying things to him that no one else can. But there was one thing even she failed to persuade him to do at the wedding and that was to dance. All the cousins were on the floor, with Harry among the most enthusiastic, but William stayed seated. He was not comfortable at the thought of dancing in front of all the other guests and nothing Zara could say or do would make him change his mind. He still enjoyed the wedding and proved that when it comes to relaxing and trusting others, like all the members of the Royal Family, they only really need and want each other.

fourteen
Royal *Pursuit*

'**W**hen you've seen your mother come home in tears because she was being pursued by bloody photographers, you can understand why I hate them so much.' – William explaining to a classmate at Eton why he disliked the media and why his feelings were so intense. In later life he admitted that 'I still don't like having to pose for cameras but when I have to do so, I do it . . . just to please my father. I look on it as a duty. That doesn't mean I enjoy it but I understand it's a necessity, a duty.'

Someone who has had the opportunity of seeing William closer than almost anyone else outside the Royal Family is the international photographer Jayne Fincher. For many years she was the favoured photographer of both Prince Charles and Princess Diana, having known both of them for over twenty years. Jayne travelled in the official party when William was taken to Australia as a baby, and later had many personal invitations to Highgrove and Kensington Palace to photograph both William and Harry. Jayne recalls one of the first photo-calls when William started at Mrs Mynor's Nursery School.

He was just three and a half and was taking part in the Christmas play. To do this the children had to cross the road to another part of the school and we were all in a special 'pen' waiting to catch a glimpse of him. As he emerged with his teachers and the other children, he was met by a phalanx of photographers and reporters all shouting out 'William'. The poor boy must

William was photographed whenever he appeared in public from the moment he was born. He was still less than a year old when the Prince of Wales carried him down the steps of the Queen's Flight aircraft at Aberdeen in 1983 to find cameras being pointed at them.

have been mystified at all the attention and wondered why everyone was calling his name. Later on I asked Diana how she had prepared him for the ordeal and she said, 'I told him the reason everyone wanted to see him was because he was a very special little boy, and if he was good I would give him some sweets.' It did the trick. Obviously Diana knew something of child psychology from the days when she worked in a nursery. We had a lovely picture of William and just behind him is a little girl showing her knickers. And I remember thinking, 'Poor girl. In years to come, someone will bring out the picture again and remind her of the day she showed her knickers to the future King.'

Something that struck Jayne as rather poignant was the way in which William, even as a three- or four-year-old, had been taught perfect manners and how to behave when he met adults. 'There was an occasion when he came off an

The Princess of Wales arrives with her two sons at Aberdeen Airport as they prepare to begin their annual summer holiday at Balmoral in August 1986.

Five-year-old William shakes hands formally with the Dean of Windsor as he arrives with his mother and other members of the Royal Family for the Christmas Day service in 1987.

aircraft of the Queen's Flight at Aberdeen on his way to Balmoral, and waiting on the tarmac were the usual group of officials. Charles and Diana shook hands with them all and then William did exactly the same thing, in precisely the same manner. It showed that Royal training begins at a very early age.'

Jayne Fincher came to know Diana and her children very well and she was gently teased when Diana discovered that Jayne's two sons are also named William and Harry. Jayne continues: 'Diana said "You're copying me aren't you?" I told her that wasn't true. We just loved the names and our choice had nothing to do with her, but I'm not sure if she believed me.' One of the characteristics that emerges from nearly all the photographs Jayne has taken of William and Harry with their mother is how tactile they all were with each other:

> I can't ever remember a single day when I saw Diana with the boys when they weren't hugging and kissing. She couldn't leave William alone. She was always fussing with his hair and touching his face. And when they went on a visit together she made sure he was all right. She was just like a mother hen. She was very affectionate towards them both and, surprisingly, so was Charles. There was no embarrassment between them. Everyone seems to think that Charles was a stiff, distant parent. From what I observed that simply was not true. He loved to have a hug, almost as much as Diana.

Princess Diana told Jayne that the reason why she paid William so much attention and made sure he was happy and knew where to stand and what to do was that when she first arrived on the Royal scene nobody gave her any help at all. She had no 'job description', did not know where to stand or sit and was not even told her position within the Royal Family. She said she was determined that her own children would never have to go through the ordeal as she had, so she taught them as much as she could from the word go. These were the days when William still enjoyed being photographed. At his nursery school, and later at Wetherby, he was quite prepared to pose as long as it did not take too long.

Opposite: To mark the fortieth birthday of the Prince of Wales in 1988, he and the Princess posed in the gardens at Highgrove with William and Harry for this formal family portrait.

On the occasion of Prince Charles's fortieth birthday, Jayne was commissioned to take some family photographs at Highgrove.

I went down a week before to see where I was going to be working and what the location was like. I was also introduced to the boys, which was a good idea because like all members of the Royal Family, they like familiar faces around them. So when the time came for the actual 'shoot' they recognized me and it made for an easier relationship all round. On the day itself, they didn't want their pictures taken – like most small boys. They wanted to go off riding their ponies that they had just been given. In addition, Diana had made them dress up in special shirts and ties which she had had made for them at Turnbull & Asser in Jermyn Street so they were not all that comfortable. The nanny was there and she was fussing around, brushing their hair and fixing

When Jayne Fincher was invited to Highgrove in August 1988 to take photographs of the children she went into a joke shop and bought some trick items to keep the boys amused. It obviously worked with William.

their ties and I thought this was going to be a disaster. So before I went down to Highgrove I called into a joke shop and bought things like fake arrows that go through the head and funny red noses that I thought would attract their attention. First of all, William decided he would be my assistant, grabbing all my equipment out of my bag, trying to set up the lights and generally causing chaos. But when he saw the joke props he had to try everything out. He put the arrow on his head and a clown's nose on, running around the garden making funny voices and showing off to his parents. They thought he was marvellous and it did the trick. I managed to get some wonderful pictures. The strange thing was that once William decided to cooperate and sit still, he made sure Harry did the same. Even at that age there was a certain something about William. It wasn't just the 'older brother' syndrome – he had a presence about him.

Some of the most informal pictures of William and Harry were taken on Sunday afternoons when they went to watch the polo matches at the Guards Polo Grounds at Windsor. On these occasions, Diana would never ask the children to sit with The Queen in the Royal Box, thinking – quite rightly – that it would be too boring for them to have to sit still all afternoon. Instead she would take them to the pony lines where they could meet some of the players and see the ponies, which is what they were interested in. Jayne Fincher recalls that on several occasions Diana also introduced her sons to a man who was unable to move because of an illness: 'Every Sunday, a man in a portable iron lung was brought by his wife to watch the polo. They would find the same place every week, right in the corner and every week, without fail, Diana would bring William and Harry to see him and have a chat. They weren't a bit put off at the sight of him and it was Diana's way of showing them how lucky they were to be able-bodied. The man and his wife were delighted to see them and they became very friendly with William and Harry.'

But these Sunday afternoons at the polo grounds also became the first occasions when William began to show his dislike of the media. 'He was thoroughly fed up with the barrage of cameras that were always pointed at him', Jayne comments 'and I remember seeing him sitting in a canvas chair, hiding his face in his hands because he didn't want his picture taken. Diana used to try and persuade him but he hated it.'

This is the kind of thing William has to face when he appears in public. A battery of photographers with long-range lenses, all determined to get that 'scoop' picture that will earn them a fortune.

The one time William did not mind having his photograph taken was when he and Harry were visiting the police, fire stations or the Army. Then they would be given specially tailored uniforms, exactly like those of the men they were visiting, and they loved dressing up – like most youngsters. There were always photo-calls on these occasions and pictures of them climbing over fire engines, sitting on police motor bikes or clambering over tanks – a particular favourite – were guaranteed front-page spreads in the newspapers and magazines.

William said that one of his most embarrassing experiences was when he was just eight years old and on his first public appearance. It was in Cardiff and hundreds of little girls of the same age crowded the streets, all trying to press bunches of flowers on him. He accepted them all and shook hands with as many as he could, but his face was bright red all the time. He still blushes easily to this day.

Jayne Fincher was again present when William really lost his cool with the press. It was during one of the early holidays in Lech in Austria when he and Harry were still learning to ski and Harry was showing off:

Harry was obviously a much more natural sportsman than William. He was swooping up and down the nursery slopes, full of confidence and loving every minute. William was much more cautious. He was nowhere near as good as Harry and he kept falling over, which is exactly what the photographers wanted to see. There were dozens of cameramen waiting, not just British but from countries all over the world. In the end, William was so fed up, he picked up his skis and walked off with his protection officer's arm around his shoulders. He'd had enough. It was the first time I'd seen it get to him, but you couldn't blame him. There were probably fifty or sixty photographers, reporters and television crews there. It was very daunting. I went back many times after that, when he became a very accomplished skier, but he never quite got over his dislike of the press. He was never comfortable when we were around.

The Royals' relationship with the press has always been ambivalent. On the one hand they demand that their press secretaries obtain the most favourable coverage whenever they attend an official function, while on the other, if a reporter or photographer catches them unawares, they are furious. And if a picture appears that has not been sanctioned – say of a member of the family in an off-duty moment – the Palace's usual complaint is that this was a 'private affair' and the photograph should not be used.

The media are often in a no-win situation because most of the time they need access to the Royals to do their jobs, unless they are working on a story about a Royal scandal, which they prefer the Palace not to know anything about until it has appeared in print. On occasions it has been known for the Palace press office to let a newspaper or broadcasting organization know that 'such and such a person is not really up to the job' or 'doesn't really fit in with what we expect of a Royal correspondent'. There is never a direct request to have the man or woman removed; the Palace would never place itself in the position where it could be accused of trying to influence coverage. But editors are clever enough to realize that if they want to continue to enjoy reasonable relations with the

Even at this age, William resembled his mother, with his blue eyes and fair hair. This picture was taken outside Clarence House and the cuff-links he is wearing were a gift from his grandfather the Duke of Edinburgh.

Opposite: *The ski resort of Klosters in Switzerland has been a regular feature of the Royal winter calendar for many years and in April 2000 there was still enough snow for the Prince of Wales and his sons to enjoy one of their favourite sports.*

Palace – and they all do – a replacement should be found as quickly and discreetly as possible.

Few members of the Royal Family have had warm feelings towards the media. The Queen Mother and Princess Diana were the only two who used them shamelessly, with the Queen Mother never falling out with photographers and Diana manipulating them when it suited her. In the latter years of her life, when she had a number of unsuitable relationships, which she tried to keep the public from hearing about, Diana blamed the media for many of her troubles. She ended up hating the press and passed this feeling on to her elder son. William has no love/hate relationship with the media; with him it appears to be entirely hate. He sees no value at all in establishing even a working, professional relationship. There are no privileged favourite scribes or photographers and when he is forced by his father into giving an interview, he is stilted and uncomfortable with little of the charm that he shows to members of the public on his rare appearances.

Prince Charles has tried very hard on a number of occasions to teach William the importance of coming to terms with the media. Charles knows better than most of his family that there is a mutual need for accommodation. The press

are not going to leave William alone simply because he does not want them around. In fact the more difficult he makes it, the more likely they are to give him a hard time. When he started at Eton Charles and Diana asked the major newspaper editors to give him some privacy, and, to be fair, they did. Throughout the five years he spent at the world's most exclusive school, he was able to have a reasonably quiet time. Then when he first went up to university at St Andrews it was agreed that, once he had posed for the obligatory photographs and answered a few questions, he would be left alone. The only group that broke the agreement was Ardent Television, the production company run by his uncle, Prince Edward, Earl of Wessex. It was also the only time that Prince Charles and his baby brother have had a stand-up row which ended with Edward apologizing to William and promising never to do it again. But he did. In August 2002, his company produced a series on British Royalty for American television which included several unsubstantiated allegations about William's private life. The series was not broadcast in Britain but it did nothing to improve relations between the young man and his uncle.

But the main reason for William's distrust of the media is that he still blames them indirectly for the death of his mother. In the final months of her life, Princess Diana frequently complained to William that journalists were making her life a misery. She knew he would always lend a sympathetic ear and she was never let down. Diana was placing an unfair burden on her son's young shoulders, but he never sought to escape from her outpourings and some of her later feelings for the press rubbed off on him and have remained to this day. He knows that he will eventually have to reach an understanding with the world's media, but at the present time there is little sign of him relaxing his attitude, which is to ignore them whenever possible and never to cooperate.

Prince Charles has often asked William to unbend a little in front of the cameras, and it is true that when they go skiing together each winter, he and Harry pose with their father in a pre-arranged photo-call. And while the pictures may look relaxed and informal, William's true feelings are not revealed. He told one of his bodyguards that there was no way he was ever going to go out of his way to help the press; why should he, he added, 'after what they have done to my mother'.

The Prince of Wales has a small but sophisticated press team based at St James's Palace but everyone knows that in recent years, ever since the death of Princess Diana, the media strings have all been pulled by one man. Mark Bolland was Prince Charles's deputy private secretary for five years, until he left in 2002 to set up his own independent public relations company – with Prince Charles as his first and most important client. His main job in the Prince's private office was to guide his employer through the turbulent years following Diana's death in 1997 and ensure that Prince Charles's public image recovered from the damage caused by the tragic events of that year. His success was outstanding. No one could have done a better job than Bolland, even though, officially, he had nothing to do with the press office. As a spin doctor he performed near miracles in transforming Charles from the most hated man in the country to a caring, affectionate single parent who was loved by his sons and who supported them on every occasion. No photo opportunity was missed and within a year Charles's reputation was restored to a level he had not enjoyed since he first married Diana in 1981. It was a remarkable transformation which not only touched the Prince of Wales and his two sons, but also included Camilla Parker Bowles, at one time the most vilified woman in the world because many people believed her to be the cause of the marriage break-up and, ultimately, the death of Diana.

But all the good work done during the past five years was destroyed overnight when Princess Diana's former butler Paul Burrell appeared in court accused of stealing hundreds of Royal items. The trial was halted sensationally when The Queen intervened personally, but the damage was done. And in the following days even more amazing revelations emerged involving the Royal Household, including a senior member of Prince Charles's personal staff, who was alleged to have sold various items belonging to his employer. The repercussions were felt around the world and the Prince of Wales's private secretary, Sir Michael Peat, was ordered to carry out a full inquiry. The media reported the story for weeks with fresh allegations almost on a daily basis. And what should have been a triumphant end to The Queen's Golden Jubilee was marred and will now be remembered as the year of the biggest scandal ever to hit the Royal Family. Even Prince William and Prince Harry were mentioned in the stories, albeit through no fault of their own, while details of Mrs Parker Bowles's role within the Prince of Wales's household caused all the old stories about her to be regurgitated. It was a public relations disaster. Some months earlier Diana's former police bodyguard Ken Wharfe wrote a 'tell-all' book about his time with

This official photocall was held in the gardens of Kensington Palace a couple of weeks before William's second birthday. At that time he did not mind meeting the press at all. His feelings towards the media would soon change.

the Princess that revealed highly personal details of her private life and the collapse of her marriage. There was enormous criticism of Wharfe in the immediate aftermath of the book being published, with most of it aimed at him because he had abused a privileged position without any consideration for the effect it would have on Diana's children. It was also another powerful reason for William to distrust the media, press and television included.

Although William's antipathy towards the media has been well documented, it has not always been the case. As an infant the television and newspaper cameras fascinated him and he was often seen running among them and asking to be shown how the equipment worked. He was intrigued by the technology and loved to chat to the cameramen and lighting technicians. By the time he was a teenager, though, all this had changed.

Like all other members of the Royal Family, William thinks the press do not have the right to intrude into his private life. However, there is a world of difference in what newspaper editors and the Palace consider is the public's right to know. The Palace believes the official duties of the Royal Family are the only areas where access should be allowed, and there is even now a Royal website giving details of such occasions. But any journalist worth his salt knows that the best stories – the ones that sell papers and the ones the public really wants to know about – are those the Palace wants to suppress.

Interest in Royalty has never wavered since The Queen came to the throne, though there have been periods of comparative 'peace' when relations between Fleet Street and the Palace have been amicable. But it was when the late Diana, Princess of Wales came on the scene it all reached fever pitch. Her picture on the cover of a magazine was guaranteed to increase sales by up to 20 per cent and 'inside' stories from 'friends' and 'Palace sources' appeared on almost a daily basis. She was the darling of the world's media and could do no wrong. And in the later years of her life when she was divorced and there was continuous speculation about her latest unsuitable male companions, the stories became more and more sensational. Thirty years earlier, Princess Margaret had been the focus of similar attention. She was the 'Diana' of her day and rarely out of the news.

These days attention is concentrated on Prince William, whom the media regard, quite rightly, as the star of the future. They need someone of his status to fill the gap left by his mother and he has the quality they are looking for. But so far William refuses to play the game. He is more 'streetwise' for his years than his father was at the same age and his staff and friends have respected his pleas for privacy.

The rest of the younger generation of Royals do not warrant anywhere near the same amount of press coverage. Photographs of the Duke of York's daughters, Princesses Beatrice and Eugenie, feature from time to time, but mainly because they are growing up, not because they are considered to be newsworthy in their own right. Lady Helen Taylor, the attractive daughter of the Duke and Duchess of Kent, also appears in magazines and newspapers, but not because of her exploits, simply because she is the outstanding beauty of the Royal Family.

When Peter and Zara Phillips, the children of the Princess Royal, were born it was expected that they would attract enormous media attention as they grew up. Fortunately for them it has not happened. Obviously the main difference between Peter and Zara and Princes William and Harry is that the Phillips children will never be required to take part in public life, which is why their mother insisted they should not have titles when they were born, even though in this she went against her own mother's express wishes. The Queen disliked the idea of any of her grandchildren being untitled, but she gave way when Anne presented very strong arguments. And the Princess has been proved right because Peter and Zara have never been subjected to the kind of pressures experienced by other young Royals of their generation. Both have lived comparatively normal lives, and the only time Zara makes the headlines is when she is involved in a public brawl with her boyfriend, with whom she later breaks up. Or because of her unconventional fashion tastes. Zara was also voted in one poll to be among the most beautiful women in the world. She showed her independence by having her tongue pierced and wearing a stud in her navel. It did not last long, but she had made her point. Peter has had even less media attention and for both this has been partly because they are a long way down the line of succession and neither is a prince or princess. If they were, their every movement would be followed and reported on by the press. People with Royal titles are newsworthy; commoners, unless they are celebrities, usually are not.

For William and Harry there will never be the slightest chance of the anonymity enjoyed by their cousins – William even more so than Harry. They both know that the slightest indiscretion will not only be featured prominently in the newspapers and on television, but will also be stored away to reappear years later when attention is focused on them for perhaps another reason.

Prince Harry already knows to his cost that, unlike most of his friends, he cannot get away with anything. In 2001, he was involved in an under-age drinking incident at a public house near Highgrove, where drugs were also being taken (which he was not accused of). Reporters and photographers flooded the place and stories appeared in every newspaper in Britain – and not just the tabloids, but the serious 'quality' broadsheets also. The story was fairly commonplace but no doubt it will reappear at frequent intervals in the future. That is what happens when you are a member of the Royal Family: Prince

Looking faintly embarrassed, William and Harry reluctantly pose for the cameras outside the main entrance to Highgrove. But they refused to put their arms around each other!

Opposite: *Prince Harry and Prince William both wearing their jubilee medals join their father at St Paul's Cathedral on 4 June 2002 during a service of thanksgiving for the Her Majesty's Golden Jubilee.*

Charles, Princess Diana, Princess Margaret, the Duke and Duchess of York and the Earl and Countess of Wessex have all discovered that where the media is concerned there is no such thing as burying the past. It always comes back to haunt you.

Looking at images of William as he grew taller, he appears to be trying to hide himself whenever he is in a group of members of the Royal Family. There are several photographs of him at the gates of Clarence House where the Queen Mother used to come out to greet the crowds on her birthday. William was always present, but although he towered over everyone else – with the

The Party at the Palace was a very successful part of the celebrations to mark The Queen's Golden Jubilee Year in 2002. But Prince William has to protect his ears from the noise of the rock bands even though his uncle the Earl of Wessex doesn't appear to be affected.

possible exception of Tim Laurence – he always tried to remain in the background and gave the impression of wishing he was somewhere else.

William's problems with the press are not going to improve until they reach an understanding, as his father did when the news of his affair with Camilla Parker Bowles became public knowledge. He is going to live under the constant scrutiny of the media and public gaze and will have to learn to cope with the attention of the world's increasingly intrusive press. If he thinks they are bad enough at the moment, things are going to get even tougher in the years to come. And not only will it be William himself whose every movement is followed and chronicled, but also his friends, particularly girlfriends, as reporters and photographers vie with each other to get that first story and picture of him in a compromising situation – or with a possible future bride.

Once Prince William leaves university it will be 'gloves off' as far as the media is concerned. Most editors feel they have played fair with William and Harry until now. They are going to demand that their reporters and photographers get the inside story and the picture they believe the world wants to see. And when you realize the sums that could be involved – Paul Burrell was said to have received £400,000 for his exclusive story from the *Daily Mirror* and ITN – the person who provides the media with advance news of William's engagement – or even a picture of his first serious girlfriend – could become rich overnight.

Even The Queen understands the need for cooperation with the press – and the damage the media can inflict on the Royal Family – as she found to her cost after the Burrell trial collapsed. Her Majesty has never underestimated the power of the media and its ability to help or hinder the monarchy. In her fifty years on the throne, she has been – in the main – on the receiving end of a very favourable press, with few exceptions, such as during the immediate aftermath of Princess Diana's death. She quickly realized that in order to regain the affection of the British people, she needed to get the media on her side. That she managed to do so successfully was a tribute to her astuteness and knowledge of how to influence public opinion. If William is to follow in his grandmother's footsteps and keep the reputation with the public he enjoys right now, he will have to learn to cope with the media – and give the impression that he enjoys doing so. Even his aunt, the Princess Royal, who was known for years as the Royal the press loved to hate – the feeling was mutual – has learned the importance of reaching an accommodation with the fourth estate. If she could do it, so must William.

fifteen
What
Next?

William has no prospects apart from his future role as King. And that may well be another thirty years away. In any case he will have to wait for both his grandmother and his father to die before he gets the job – not the most encouraging outlook for a young man at the start of the twenty-first century. When his father was his age, he found the destiny that faced him rather bleak, but he knew there was no alternative, so he buckled down to the never-ending round of public duties that has been his lot to the present day.

William is a bright, clever person who, for the foreseeable future, will shoulder the burden of being a Prince of the Realm. It is a title that does not mean a great deal to the average young person in Britain and even less so to those abroad. The only people to whom it is important – apart from the Royal Family of course, and the hardcore of ardent monarchists – are those social climbers who aspire to belong to the exclusive group that surrounds this most celebrated family.

What lies ahead for William is a life of privilege and power. He will never have to worry about money. Apart from the fortune he will inherit when he becomes Prince of Wales, he was left a large sum from his mother's reported £17-million will and he has a trust fund, which was set up for him by The Queen when he was born.

William will never know what it is like to have to make his own way in life, much as he might choose to if, indeed, such a choice were possible. Not for him the thrill of seeing an ambition achieved, nor the pain of failure. It must be stultifying

A young Prince William with Princes Diana's police bodyguard, Inspector Ken Wharfe, who after he left the Royalty Protection Department wrote a controversial book about his life at her side.

for someone of his intelligence. There is nothing William can do that will alter the path that has been chosen for him. Just imagine chatting with your friends at school and university, with them all getting excited about the future and the jobs they are going to get; the worlds they are going to conquer, the fortunes they are going to make, and you have to sit there taking no part in the discussions because it has all been decided for you from the moment you were born. It is a daunting prospect for a young man on the threshold of adulthood but one that he would no more consider abandoning than he would of becoming the first Royal astronaut. In fact there is more chance of him taking off into space than giving up his heritage. As Chris Patten comments;

He may not be able to have the same level of ambition of those young men and women without that burden of dynastic responsibility, but he can have

Wherever William goes, there is always a crowd of admirers. These children are giving him a present after watching him play polo at the Beaufort Club in 2002.

ambitions about his personal development. He can have ambitions about various causes, as his father does. The recent controversy about Prince Charles writing to ministers is ludicrous. I would far rather have members of the Royal Family who are interested in important issues and prepared to try and make a difference than not. He can also have more personal ambitions than his father was able to have at the same age because society is becoming much more tolerant of the idea of Royalty having a professional career, perhaps in a similar sense as the Danish princes have. He is blessed in that he carries into the limelight a remarkable number of personal attributes: good looks, charm, intelligence, with a touch of charisma and given the amount of attention he is going to continue to attract from a voracious media, what he needs to add to those qualities is a thick skin. If he does that, he won't go far wrong.

William on one of his walkabouts – this time in The Mall outside Buckingham Palace on 4 June 2002 during the celebrations to mark The Queen's Golden Jubilee.

When he eventually succeeds to the throne it will be as King William V, if he chooses to keep his own name. He does not have to of course; his father is said to have chosen the name George, in honour of his grandfather, George VI, when he comes to the throne. The last monarch to bear the name William, King William IV, the third son of George III, ascended the throne at the age of sixty-four in 1830. Neither father nor son was particularly successful as sovereign: George III is remembered as the King who gave away the American colonies – and for his supposed madness – while William IV was sometimes called 'Silly Billy' because of his habit of making spontaneous promotions in the Royal Navy in his role as Lord High Admiral when he was still Duke of Clarence.

The future William V is very different from his ancestor in that his training has been to prepare him to rule in a modern world where the monarch's word is no longer law. Although he will have the right to use the Royal prerogative, he already knows that, like his grandmother and father before him, he will be required to work within the rules of parliamentary democracy. If Elizabeth II is anything to go by, William will learn that his influence may be massive but his actual power severely limited. Perhaps the most important of the sovereign's powers remains the right to choose a Prime Minister in the event of a hung Parliament, and even to dismiss the Prime Minister and dissolve Parliament. However, no sovereign has done this since William IV discharged Lord Melbourne in 1834, and it is unlikely that any monarch in the future would care to risk repeating this action. But Lord Blake says it is vital that the monarch retains this power: 'The Queen is the guardian of constitutional legitimacy in the broadest sense of the words. She cannot be this without possessing, in addition to influence and prestige, however great, some ultimate powers of last resort.'

Lord Blake also believes that in preserving its monarchy, Britain has been saved from the possibility of a dictatorship. He explained to me that countless surveys on the constitutional position of the sovereign have shown that if the views of The Queen were seen to be in conflict with her Prime Minister, a substantial majority believed The Queen's opinion would – and should – prevail. He went on to say, though, that in a sense we do not need a monarchy at all. 'It is not a necessary feature of a western type of modern democracy.' Those European countries that have retained a monarchy, have sovereigns with vastly different roles to that in Britain. For example, the King of Spain attends Cabinet

One of William's greatest assets is his ability to get on with people of all ages and from all walks of life. Here he is chatting with members of the Royal Old Age Pensioners Club in Glasgow in September 2001 just before he started at university.

What Next?

All eyes were on William as he strolled among the crowds at a garden party at the Palace of Holyroodhouse in Edinburgh in 2002.

meetings, which would never be tolerated in Britain. In Sweden, the sovereign no longer has the right to appoint a Prime Minister, while in Belgium, every member of the Royal Family, including the sovereign, has a job. It has been well documented that there is a tradition of abdication within the Royal House of the Netherlands, but putting aside the single instance of 1936 when Edward VIII gave up his throne to marry Mrs Wallis Simpson, Britain has not considered this option. If The Queen lives to be 100 she will reign for all that time.

William is expected to play an increasingly prominent role in the life of the Royal Family in the years to come and he accepts this, albeit somewhat reluctantly at the present time. Already moves are being made to ensure that his first public appointments will be suitable and popular. He is being talked about as the next Prior for the Order of St John in Wales, which would be very popular in the Principality and not too demanding as an introduction to Royal duties in his own right. William would mainly be a figurehead with a deputy carrying out most of the work. There is a precedent for having a member of the Royal Family as Head of the Order in Wales as the Duke of Windsor, when he was Prince of Wales, accepted the position. The overall Sovereign Head is The Queen, while the Grand Prior is the Duke of Gloucester, so Royal connections are very strong with the Order of St John. Another official post might be as Vice-patron of the Welsh Rugby Union (The Queen is Patron). His mother was adopted as an unofficial team mascot and we have seen how much she and her sons enjoyed supporting the national side at the Millennium Stadium in Cardiff. Besides, just as his late mother did before him, William captures the public's imagination. They need a star and he is it. No other member of the family, with his father now a middle-aged man and his grandmother, The Queen, not too far off eighty, has the charisma and charm necessary to engage the attention of a sceptical people who are nevertheless hungry for a new hero. He is very much his own man and has matured into a strong and confident young adult with the style of his late mother and discipline and self-control of the House of Windsor – a powerful combination.

Prince Charles once said that the realization that he was next in line to the throne hit him as a 'ghastly, inexorable sense'. And he has had two very difficult tasks facing him in recent years. He has had to convince the British people that he is the right man to become the next King, following the scandals of his divorce and subsequent personal revelations, and also that he is a good father to his two sons. That he has managed to achieve excellent results on both counts is a tribute to Charles's dedication and devotion to duty in the face of considerable criticism. William will not have to face these problems. He enjoys the advantage of enormous public goodwill, and many people already believe that, in the years to come, he will make an excellent sovereign.

At a time when the monarchy is being attacked from many sides and when countries within the Commonwealth, which have traditionally supported having the British sovereign as their head of state, are now increasingly turning towards republicanism, William might be excused for questioning whether he will eventually inherit the throne. Indeed, will there still be a throne to occupy when his time comes? And how much support will there be for a monarchy, even in Britain, in twenty or thirty years from now?

The Prince of Wales is accompanied by Camilla Parker Bowles at a Prince's Foundation Gala Dinner in London in June 2000. The dinner raised thousands of pounds for the Prince's charity and Camilla's presence ensured maximum publicity for the event.

As an intelligent young man with an enquiring mind, these questions must already have occurred to William. He has discussed the problems with his father and probably also with The Queen. She has an unquestioned belief in the continuity of the monarchy and an unshakeable faith that her role, and that of her heirs, will survive whatever upheavals may follow in the years to come. Others are not so sanguine.

William has already shown that he is an independent person who likes to take his own decisions. That is a trait Royalty discourages and he will no doubt have it tested as the years go by. Palace courtiers have noticed his tendency to speak his mind and they fear that his independence shows more than a streak of the temperament he has inherited from his mother, and sense potential problems in the future from her son.

As a modern young Royal, William has been fortunate in having much more freedom than any previous member of the family. He is allowed to choose his own friends, even if realistically they nearly all come from highly privileged backgrounds. So he is hardly likely to socialize with boys and girls from the local comprehensive schools. He is often found in the company of attractive young women who are members of the social elite. They are 'safe' and can be relied on to know the 'form' as their parents and grandparents all come from similar upper-class families. So there is no danger that any of them would place William in a compromising situation, even when he visits one of the trendy nightclubs he enjoys. His position within the Royal Family guarantees a glamorous appeal, and this, combined with his casual good looks and unstudied, easy charm, is already proving irresistible to young women throughout the world. But he has never had, nor will he ever be allowed to have, the kind of informal date that most young people of his age take for granted.

Behind everything William does, the people he meets, the places he visits, one object remains in mind, his continual preparation for kingship. Both The Queen and Prince Charles are determined that nothing will stand in the way of that. He is undoubtedly the star of the future; the one on whom the Royal Family's hopes rest. Their agenda is clear and simple: bring William along slowly and carefully, so that by the time he is thirty – and The Queen will be eighty-six – he will have the confidence, the willingness and, more importantly, the ability to take over the reins of monarchy whenever he is required.

The future king-to-be practising his regal wave from one of the Royal coaches during The Queen's Golden Jubilee.

Index

Index

Index